# Healing From Family Trauma

— . —

## A Guidebook for Adult Children of Toxic Parents

## Christine A Fisher BSN RNC

### Bio Bandit Publishing

## Disclaimers:

Please note the information contained within this document is for educational and entertainment purposes only. All effort has been executed to present accurate, up to date, reliable, complete information. No warranties of any kind are declared or implied. Readers acknowledge that the author is not engaged in the rendering of legal, financial, medical or professional advice. The content within this book has been derived from various sources. Please consult a licensed professional before attempting any techniques outlined in this book.

By reading this document, the reader agrees that under no circumstances is the author responsible for any losses, direct or indirect, that are incurred as a result of the use of the information contained within this document, including, but not limited to, errors, omissions, or inaccuracies.

This book may bring up some strong feelings and subsequent discomfort. It is not intended to make anyone feel like a bad parent or bad child, or to have you relive these experiences without the assistance needed to properly process your emotions.

Sections of this book cover fictional scenarios for illustrative purposes. Names, characters, places, and incidents are either the product of the author's imagination or used fictitiously, and any resemblance to actual persons, living or dead, business establishments, events, or locales is entirely coincidental.

BIG
BANDIT
PUBLISHING

As a way of saying thank you for your purchase,
Take the Adverse Childhood Events (ACE) Quiz to score
your personal level of childhood trauma and determine
what that score actually means.

Free ACEs Quiz

Simply visit:
https://www.healingfromfamilytrauma.com
or use the above link

# CONTENTS

# INTRODUCTION

*Jamie strips herself down and stares at her reflection. She started drinking beer three hours ago, and judging by the fact that she has another waiting six feet away, on her nightstand, she has plans of continuing.*

*Her shaky hands poke and prod at her stomach. She grabs a piece of fat and shakes it, hard. In her mind, no 28 year old should look like this. No human alive should look like this. Her doctor has been trying to get her to lose weight for years, but to no avail.*

*A tightness begins in her chest. She attempts to grab at it, but cannot reach it. Jamie falls to her knees and rests her forehead on the ground. She wants to disappear.*

$$\cdot \; \cdot \; \bullet \; \cdot \; \bullet \; \cdot \; \bullet \; \cdot \; \bullet \; \cdot \; \cdot$$

Let me guess: If you relate to this, you may suffer from low self-esteem, unfulfilling interpersonal relationships, and a variety of different physical and mental problems such as anxiety, depression, or obesity? These are common effects that are caused from traumatic childhood events. About 21 million individuals who are currently diagnosed with depression went through a traumatic event during their childhood ("Fast facts," 2021). How do we prevent these negative effects? How do we even know that any problems you are facing are occurring due to childhood traumas? It's time to find out.

## What This Book is About

This book is designed to inform and help guide the healing process for individuals who believe they may have experienced an adverse childhood event during their youth. Each chapter goes over something different, covering such topics as

- Insight into why one might be struggling with the effects of childhood trauma as an adult
- What the mental and the physical effects of childhood trauma can look like in an adult
- Different types of therapy available to those suffering from the lasting effects of childhood trauma
- Signs that therapy is needed
- What not to do in order to heal from trauma
- Actionable steps to take in self-care
- Developing a mental health routine that can improve resiliency
- What can be done to improve your parent relationship, if so desired.

This book isn't just about reading about trauma or complaining about bad parents. This book is a call to action to start the healing process through actionable steps that can be taken.

## Is This Book for Me?

I wrote this book specifically for adult children of toxic parents. An adult who reads this may or may not be aware of the toxicity of their parents, because a lot of toxic behavior can be subtle but nonetheless damaging. These adults might be suffering from symptoms of trauma from adverse childhood events, such as anxiety, depression, poor coping mechanisms, emotional outbursts, apathy, trouble with relationships, and more. Maybe you might have been recommended this book by a close friend. Whatever the reason you find yourself reading this, I am sure that it will help you.

If you find yourself battling one of the listed issues stemming from unresolved childhood trauma, this book is for you.

If you are searching for answers or trying to work on a positive relationship with your parents, this book is for you.

If you are a parent yourself with a history of trauma and are looking for ways to become a better parent for your children, this book is for you.

I also realize that it may not be the suffering individual that is the one reading this. Therefore, I have created this content so that it can be helpful to anyone who wants to help a close family member or friend work through their trauma or better understand what they are going through.

Ultimately, I want to empower as many people as possible in taking control of their life by giving them the tools and resources necessary to transcend childhood trauma and the negative effects associated with it.

## How This Book Will Benefit You

This book offers a framework for healing; the information provided will guide you to better understand yourself, show you how to cultivate self-love, and increase your coping skills and techniques for dealing with trauma. With the multitude of health effects associated with being the child of a toxic parent, you cannot afford to avoid taking action. This is my call to action to motivate you to take charge of your health and well-being.

Through learning about the effects and risks associated with adverse childhood events, you will begin to understand the best course of action for your individual healing journey. You will learn that positive self-care steps can be taken to effectively reduce the negative effects of your childhood experiences. You will learn to acknowledge that you are worth it, and deserve to be loved unconditionally.

Self-love, self-compassion, self-care, self-acceptance, and self-worth are all important concepts we will cover in order to increase your resilience in life, the benefit being that symptoms of adverse childhood events will be significantly reduced.

And if so desired, you can begin the process of learning to repair a relationship with a toxic parent. However, this is only offered as a last optional step. First and foremost, this book is intended to benefit your own well-being and relationships with yourself.

## How to Use This Book

This book is not meant as a reference guide to sit on your shelf until you need help with a specific problem. In order to use this book and receive the most benefits, please read in order from chapter one to chapter ten. Each chapter builds on the information provided in the previous chapter. In culmination, you will receive all the knowledge necessary to begin healing from your trauma.

Are you ready to begin the process of healing and learning how to improve our mental and physical well-being? Read on to chapter one to begin your healing journey.

# 1

## THE ORIGIN OF FAMILY TRAUMA

The effects of family trauma can be lifelong for many people, but that doesn't mean progress cannot be made toward healing. This book is designed to help individuals who have gone through childhood trauma start their healing process, as they are at high risk for negative physical and mental conditions throughout adulthood. I want to create a positive framework for healing.

Adults who have gone through family trauma at a young age may be confused as to whether or not their experiences are actually valid. Sometimes, they may wonder if their experiences even happened at all. How does one go about figuring out this information? It can be hard and confusing looking back at old memories and trying to determine what was good parenting versus what was bad parenting. In this first chapter, we will take a look at what a toxic parent is, and how you can know if you may have had one.

## Toxic Parents

Parents are supposed to be the frontline protectors of the nuclear family. In a perfect world, parents wouldn't make any mistakes while raising their children. Children would always feel safe around their parents and come to them for everything. Unfortunately, as much as this image gets ingrained in our heads, not every parent actually acts in such a manner. In reality, there are some parents in the world that are truly bad parents. They have a child and then put that child under dreadful living circumstances. Sometimes, they are not always motivated by the right reasons to have children. They themselves are often not fit or prepared to be raising a child, and the child has to suffer the long-term consequences in return.

I used the word "bad" to describe the people who parent in such a manner. Can there be a bad parent without toxicity being involved? There are other forms of bad relationships that are separated from their toxic forms. A bad romantic relationship doesn't necessarily always mean that it was a toxic relationship. In terms of parents, the terms "bad" and "toxic" are used interchangeably. There is a huge difference between a bad parent and a bad significant other. With a bad parent, you are in the period of your life where you are rapidly developing and you are the most impressionable. Everything they do has an impact on how you grow into your own person. A bad significant other can be interpreted as they were bad for you personally. Incompatibility does not equate toxicity. Perhaps the two of you had different love languages, and it didn't work out in that sense. This just isn't transferable to a familial relationship in the same way.

While it isn't possible to simply be a bad parent, it is possible to be a good parent with some bad traits. There could be a good parent who is taken aback by their child wanting to go down a different career path than what they personally saw for them, and they don't take it very well. This parent can learn to accept over a short period of time, possibly a few weeks or even up to a few months, that the child is incredibly passionate about this particular career path, and supports them during their endeavors. The parent's initial shock and disapproval doesn't immediately negate all of the love and caring that they have shown throughout the years, although it will certainly make some sort of an impact on the child. The key is coming back from the bad parenting and learning from previous mistakes.

Toxic parents, on the other hand, have multiple bad parenting habits, and while some may have tried to make a change, they did not succeed. Sometimes, the toxic parent manages to make the change years after the child has transitioned into adulthood, but by that time, the consequences have already done their damage.

Oftentimes, it can be difficult to discern if one truly had a toxic parent. Childhood already contains so many foggy memories, and incidents of trauma can be even harder to remember. What you think might have happened could have been a false memory you believe to be true because your parents managed to make the change to become better after you had already grown into adulthood. You could've experienced gaslighting to make your experiences of childhood trauma seem invalidated. If you believe that you may have had a toxic parent growing up, you owe it to yourself to investigate your memories. You might find a lot of answers to the questions you never knew that you had.

## Define: Who Are They?

Toxic parents are not all alike, although there are some general characteristics and behaviors that they may have. Any toxic parent could have any combination of these general characteristics and behaviors: putting blame on the child, being overly controlling, comparing the child to others, guilt tripping the child, disregarding the child's wants and needs, manipulation, creating unreasonable demands, competing with the child, and overreacting to things the child does. All of these characteristics and behaviors create long-term negative effects during the child's time of development, in turn, impacting them throughout their adult life.

Toxic parents are known to be emotionally immature. This can otherwise be known as having the clinical diagnosis of narcissistic personality disorder. This is not to say that all toxic parents are narcissistic, nor are all parents with narcissistic personality disorder toxic parents. However, in combination with having children, having untreated or undiagnosed narcissistic personality disorder can lead to becoming a toxic parent due to the symptoms of narcissistic personality disorder. Symptoms of narcissistic personality disorder that can affect children being raised in that environment include: lack of empathy, hypersensitivity to criticism, undermining other's confidence in order to boost their own, putting their own needs first, focusing on their immediate demands, and being naive to the consequences of their actions.

If by just reading these characteristics and behaviors of a toxic parent you're getting a familiar feeling in your gut, then you might've had a toxic parent. If you still aren't quite sure, let's look deeper to see if we can make sense of what exactly a toxic parent is.

## How to Know If You Have Had One

*Ever since her mother got them, Jamie loved to look at the glass fish that were placed on the mantle. They were so shiny and so colorful. Six in total, Jamie named them all. She longed to play with them one day. They would make an excellent addition to her underwater world she made with her LEGO set. Her mother didn't like Jamie being near them, though. She had been scolded multiple times for simply being in the same room as the tiny glass fish.*

*But Jamie had just turned eight, and she believed that she was finally old enough to be worthy of the fish. She had her eyes set on the bright purple fish she called Chrissy Fish. If she could just reach a little further, a little further, a little further...*

*"Jamie!" her mother shrieked. Hearing her mother startled her, and she knocked Chrissy Fish over. The brilliant purple glass turned into millions of brilliant purple shards.*

*"Oh, you little brat! You selfish little brat!" her mother yelled. Jamie felt tears begin to well up in her eyes. "You don't have a reason to be crying here. If anyone should be crying, it should be me! You just broke my priceless 1987 collector's piece. At this rate, I should just keep you in your room to keep you from messing anything else up." She snatched Jamie's arm and led her out of the room. Jamie's hand hurt from where the glass gave her a small cut.*

Putting the blame on the child can mean one of two things. It can come in the form of a genuine accident occurring or the parent making a mistake and then the blame for the accident or mistake getting put on the child. A young boy who forgets to clean his room due to genuine forgetfulness, not because he did not want to do it, should not get blamed and punished as it was an accident. A little girl breaking a dish while trying to set the table should not take the blame, as there is no blame that needs to be placed.

Toxic parents are oftentimes overly controlling of their children. This can look like controlling aspects of the child's life that wouldn't normally need input from the parent, or aspects that may have needed input earlier on, but don't need it as the child grows older. When the child is a teenager, the parent no longer needs to tell the child what to wear, no longer needs to control their finances in its entirety, set up times for when the child can see their friends, and other similar behaviors. In general, the parent never needs to control who the child is friends with, if the child gets to eat a meal or not (if the family is financially stable enough to have all three meals), and whether or not the child is allowed to work on schoolwork at a certain time.

Comparing the child to other children is when the parent looks at an attribute their child has and states that another child that they both know is doing something better in relation to that same attribute. For instance, this could be the parent saying that the neighbor's child is smarter, or that their cousin is kinder. The parent could also compare skills, such as saying that one kid is better at drawing than another kid is.

If you've ever heard your parent say something along the lines of "I have clothed you, housed you, and fed you" in order to get you to do something, that is guilt tripping. It is a tactic used to make the child feel guilty in order to make them do something that the parent wants. This could be getting the child to stop complaining or getting the child to perform some kind of task for the parent. Guilt tripping comes in forms other than what is listed above, but the overall idea is that the parent will bring up something that they have done for the child in order to get them to do something for them.

Disregarding the child's wants and needs can be dangerous. If you've ever been denied food, water, medicine, or shelter, you have been denied a need by your parent. If you've ever been denied entertainment such as television, books, video games, toys, the ability to go outside, or the ability to see friends, you have been denied a want by your parent. These needs and wants are essential for a child to grow in a healthy environment.

Similar to guilt tripping, manipulation is a tactic used by toxic parents in order to get a child to do what they want. This is a wide topic that includes lying, gaslighting, threatening, withholding information, and emotionally abusing someone. Essentially, it is meant to change someone's perception of certain events. This can be seen as a toxic parent telling the child that an event was not as bad as they remember it, which invalidates their experience of it. It could also be seen as them threatening to hurt the child if they told anyone about it.

Being asked to perform an unreasonable task for your age is just that: unreasonable. What defines absurd? Think about your capabilities for the different ages you were growing up. It wouldn't be absurd to ask a five-year old to clean up their toys, but it would be absurd to have them make dinner. It wouldn't be outlandish to ask your child in the seventh grade their advice on which shoes look better with a certain outfit, but it would be outlandish to have them give you advice when you're having marital issues.

Competition with the child can mean that the parent views their child as a threat to an aspect of their life that needs to be brought down. This is where a parent undermines the child's achievements and raises up their own. Imagine if you were incredibly excited to come in third at your school's spelling bee, only for your parent to tell you that they had gotten second place. If you had gotten a 3.50 GPA in high school. Your parent would follow that up by saying that they had gotten a 3.75 GPA.

The last characteristic and behavior to look out for in a toxic parent is if they overreact. Going back to the example of if a little girl breaks a dish while setting the table, the girl should not be met with extreme punishment such as having to go without dinner. The parent should not scream and yell at the child in reaction to the accident. What the child did and how the parent reacts in the situation do not match in the slightest.

If you recognize any of these situations, know that you are not alone. Unfortunately, toxic parents are common, but it is important to note that even if you have experienced any of the above, you are worthy of unconditional love in all regards. There are many resources outside of just this book that are helpful to the healing process and that are widely available to you. You are taking the right first steps to creating a positive self-worth.

## Adverse Childhood Events (ACEs): What They Are

Toxic parenting can lead to an adverse childhood event (ACE). An ACE is a traumatic event that occurs between the ages of birth to 17 years of age. The events that fall under the category of an ACE vary, but can include violence, health conditions, and abuse. ACEs can cause several different physical and mental health problems later in adulthood based on the effects of the trauma.

The sad truth of the matter is that 61% of adults living in the United States have reported experiencing at least one ACE during their childhood ("Fast facts," 2021). While this evidences the fact that you are not alone in your struggles, it shows that something that shouldn't ever happen occurs for more than half of all children. Some individuals are more likely to experience an ACE due to being a part of a gender or racial minority group.

The number of individuals who have gone through an ACE is large, but there is hope for every single one of them. Healing is not an easy process, but it is a necessary one. Necessary and possible. To continue on, it's time to further your understanding of adverse childhood events and touch on the negative effects they can have going into adulthood if they go unresolved.

# 2

## ADVERSE CHILDHOOD EVENTS

*Jamie was sitting at the dining table, eating her fourth bowl of fettuccine. Her stomach ached, but the creamy sauce comforted her. Her boyfriend, Ken, sat across the table from her. They sat in silence. He had finished eating by her second bowl, and he was now doing something on his phone. Jamie longed for a connection, a spark, but she didn't feel anything there anymore. She wasn't sure if it was there to begin with.*

*"Did you want dessert?" she asked.*

*"Babe, can you let me finish this article before you try talking to me?" he replied.*

*She stared at her pasta bowl. She should've known better than to try to talk to him right now. Of course he was busy. Her appetite dissipated. She stood up to take her bowl to the sink, her chair squeaking against the floor.*

*Ken slammed his fist on the table. "What is your freaking deal? I told you I wanted to finish the article!"*

*Jamie let out a little whimper. Suddenly, she was 10 again. Sitting at her family's kitchen table was her, her mother, and her father. Her mother and father were talking about something when Jamie interrupted.*

*"Daddy! I saw a really cool bird today. I think you'd really like it."*

*Her father didn't turn his head. "Jamie, what did we discuss about speaking when not spoken to?"*

*"It's not polite?"*

*"That's right. And what happens when we do things that aren't polite?"*

*"I have to learn my lesson."*

*"That's right. Now go pick out the wooden spoon you believe to be fitting of the punishment."*

## List of Adverse Childhood Events

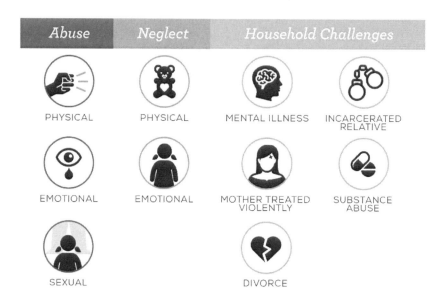

There are 10 total adverse childhood events that an individual can possibly go through. You could have experienced more than one event during your childhood. Each ACE is different and can cause different traumas. What are the 10 ACEs?

The first ACE is physical abuse. If an adult in your home ever laid hands on you in a way that was meant to cause you harm, that was physical abuse. This can be in the form of slapping, punching, grabbing you, or even using objects to cause you physical harm. Typically, these acts would leave marks or some form of physical injury that others would be able to see.

The second ACE is sexual abuse. If anyone who was at least 5 years older than you laid hands on you in a sexual way, that was sexual abuse. This includes the older individual touching your body, having you touch their body, attempting oral sex, or attempting penetrative sex with you. Not only would it be considered sexual abuse, but if the older individual succeeded in their attempt in penetrative sex, that would be considered statutory rape.

The third ACE is emotional abuse. If an adult in your home made you feel lesser than you were, that was emotional abuse. Emotional abuse goes hand in hand with manipulation. It includes threatening, swearing at, and knocking down the child's self-esteem. This type of abuse often leads the child to believe that they will be physically abused.

The fourth type of ACE is physical neglect. If your physical needs were often not met, that was physical neglect. This includes not being taken to the doctor when needed, not living in a clean environment, not having food and water, and not having protection. Physical neglect can be particularly rough on a child because they have no means to be able to get these physical needs from outside sources. The adults in the household are typically the only ones able to provide for them at that moment in time.

The fifth type of ACE is emotional neglect. If your emotional needs were often not met, that was emotional neglect. This can look like not feeling like you had someone in the family that you could safely come to when you had emotional turmoil. If you ever felt like you were unloved, like you were unimportant, or that you didn't have anything to gain from your family, that also falls under emotional neglect.

The sixth type of ACE is if a member of your household had a debilitating mental illness. If at any point in time someone in your household was diagnosed with a mental illness that also outwardly affected you, that was this ACE. This could be anything from a mood disorder such as major depressive disorder, to a personality disorder, such as narcissistic personality disorder. Under this specific ACE is also whether or not anyone in your household self-harmed or attempted suicide during your time there.

The seventh type of ACE is if your parents were separated or divorced. This includes if your parents had ended up reconciling, or getting remarried to other people eventually.

The eighth ACE is substance abuse. If anyone in your household had ever used drugs, such as depressants, stimulants, or hallucinogens, to the point where they had become dependent on the drug, that was substance abuse. This includes alcoholism. Substance abuse in a household often affects the chance of an individual going through other ACEs. For instance, alcohol can increase aggression in some people who drink it, increasing the chance of physical or emotional abuse. The money that goes to buying the drugs can take away from other needs, such as new clothes or much needed school supplies, increasing the chance of physical neglect.

The ninth ACE is whether or not violence has been performed against your mother. If your mother's significant other, such as her boyfriend or her husband, ever threatened to hurt her or physically abused her, that was violence performed against your mother. The same actions that can be categorized under the ACE of physical abuse can be categorized under this one as well, including if the person doing the violent acts had a weapon or not.

The last ACE is if there was a member of your household who has been incarcerated. If someone you lived with was ever sent to jail or prison for any amount of time, that was them being incarcerated.

## ACE Questionnaire

Reading through all of the descriptions of the different ACEs can be overwhelming, especially if you have experienced one or more of them. In depth descriptions might bring back bad memories you didn't even know that you had. If you feel like your head is swimming reading through what the different ACEs are, there is an online questionnaire that you can take that essentially tells you how many ACEs you have gone through for you.

A simple Google search can help you find an ACE questionnaire online, but I recommend using the free ACE quiz that I have created found at HealingfromFamilyTrauma.com.

The quiz simplifies the ACEs in a way that is easy to understand, and at the same time, calculates how many ACEs you have experienced. Each point you have on the questionnaire represents one ACE you have gone through. In other words, the more points you have, the more adverse childhood events you have lived through, and the more at risk you are for health conditions throughout your adult life.

While the ACE questionnaire is great for helping individuals figure out how many ACEs they have lived through, it does have a few flaws. The questionnaire only takes into account the bad things that have occurred during one's childhood, and leaves all of the good things that may have built up resilience behind. These events that have increased resilience are a part of the healing process, so they patch up some of the damage done by ACEs. There are some people who have minimal long-term effects of their ACEs because they had built resilience during the same time they went through those events.

The questionnaire also does not take into account any other predispositions to health conditions that an individual may have. Yes, you are more likely to become overweight if you have experienced an ACE, but there could also be the possibility that obesity runs in your family. Perhaps you have a diet that is primarily fats and sugars, which makes you chronically fatigued, rather than this being an effect from your ACEs.

When starting your path of healing, it is important to keep all factors in mind. You may focus a lot on moving forward from the events that occurred in the past, but if they weren't the only causes for your health conditions, then you aren't automatically going to get better. It's best to investigate your life to make sure that you have all your bases covered. Look into your genetic history, your diet, and your substance intake to make sure that you're treating every part of your mind, body, and soul. Try to keep in mind as you read that it is quite difficult to avoid all ACEs, which is why I have chosen to focus on the path of increasing resilience and the promotion of trauma healing, in addition to awareness and prevention.

It's also important to note that if you are currently a parent, you need to hang in there and believe in yourself. Being a parent is hard work, especially after personally suffering from childhood trauma. Every parent makes mistakes, but that doesn't mean you are a bad parent putting your child through an ACE. For instance, getting a divorce is a better decision than staying in an abusive relationship that could potentially cause more trauma for your child. It's important that you hang in there and focus on your resiliency training—something we'll cover much later in this book.

## Results of ACEs in Individuals

*Jamie is 12-years old. She is packing her backpack to spend the weekend at her father's house. Clothes, books, her phone, a charger. Almost forgot! She peaks underneath her bed to find her stash of emergency food. He always works on the weekends, and never provides enough food for Jamie to eat while she's there. She grabs some granola bars, instant macaroni cups, and a few oatmeal packets. It wasn't much, but it would have to do.*

*"Jamie! Hurry up, you're going to make us late again! It's bad enough that we have to see your piece of crap father," her mother called from down the stairs. She stomps away from the stairs and slams the front door shut. Jamie flinches, and takes a second to breathe.*

*She'll have to ask Mrs. Norberry next door for some more food when she gets back to her mother's house. The emergency food supply is running low. As much as she hates to admit it, she hopes that her mom wins full custody. Having to ask for food so consistently, only to go hungry so often, is practically a nightmare.*

*"Jamie? Hey, you doing okay?" She feels a tap on her shoulder. Jamie is 37-years old, and has accidentally fallen asleep at her work desk.*

*She offers a tiny smile to the coworker who woke her up. "Sorry about that. I didn't get a lot of sleep last night. Thanks for looking out for me before the boss came in."*

Physical Changes in the Brain

When ACEs occur, there is a chance that it could cause a physical change within the brain during the child's development. It may be hard to believe, but it's true. The brain of someone who has endured at least one ACE physically looks different than of those who did not go through such an experience. In what ways?

To begin, the hippocampus is smaller in adults who lived through an ACE. This part of the brain is known to play a huge role in memory functions. Besides just memory, the hippocampus also processes emotions and helps with stress management within the brain. If the hippocampus is smaller in these adults, what exactly does that mean?

Recent research has found that hippocampus shrinkage has been linked to severe stress, and furthermore, post-traumatic stress disorder (PTSD) (Gilbertson et al, 2010). The exact impact that a small hippocampus has on the likelihood that an individual will develop PTSD has yet to be determined. Since PTSD is caused by someone going through a traumatic event, it is unlikely that the relationship between a small hippocampus and PTSD is causational. However, it could be correlational. If the hippocampus helps with stress management processes, then a smaller hippocampus could potentially be less effective, making the body more vulnerable to severe stress events that cause PTSD. It could also be correlational in the sense that individuals who have been through ACEs have developed PTSD from those events, and they also have smaller hippocampi from the same event.

Besides causing the hippocampus to not reach its full estimated size, living through one or more ACE also affects gray matter content in individuals. What role does gray matter play, and why is it so important?

Gray matter is where the neurons of the brain are located. These neurons are in charge of sending messages throughout the brain. They tell the body if they perceive something in one of the sensory fields, such as in vision, audition, olfaction, and gustation. Neurons are in control of thoughts, feelings, behaviors, essentially every action that takes place within the brain.

When someone experiences at least one ACE, they are likely to develop less gray matter in certain parts of their brain. Specifically, the amygdala and the prefrontal cortex. The brain structure known as the amygdala processes emotions, particularly fear. It is also used to detect any potential threatening stimuli that is in the immediate area. The prefrontal cortex is in charge of many different cognitive functions. It helps the hippocampus with aspects of memory, while also contributing toward how we prepare for future events, how we pay attention, and how we express emotions physically.

Together, the amygdala and prefrontal work to figure out what threats the amygdala detects are real and which ones are false alarms. With less gray matter devoted to these areas, there are less neurons working this job. Therefore, false alarms are going to be more prevalent, increasing the chance of someone experiencing anxiety in their daily life.

## Mental and Physical Effects

Due to the complexity of the brain and how many different cognitive functions it has, there are several general effects ACEs can cause that can develop into more specific health issues later on down the line. All of the functions of the hippocampus, amygdala, and prefrontal cortex will be affected, past what we've already discussed. Since both the hippocampus and the prefrontal cortex deal with memory in some form, memory overall can worsen. Impulsivity has been known to increase as the ability to self-regulate decreases. In contrast, the ability to make decisions also decreases, which can affect the area in life of the person's responsibilities, but encourage their impulses. Lastly, as previously mentioned, stress management is affected to the point where it is harder for the brain to handle stressful situations.

These problems with cognitive function create further health conditions. If someone is having trouble with stress management due to damage to brain structures, they have the possibility of developing chronic stress. There are numerous different health conditions that can stem from chronic stress, such as heart disease, migraines, and depression. Increased impulsivity can lead to the possibility of substance use. If not careful, the use of substances can eventually lead to a substance use disorder, which can lead to many different physical and mental effects depending on the substance used. Just these effects don't even begin to cover the full list of possibilities, but hopefully it gives you a general idea of how serious it can be.

While all of these effects are possibilities, it is important to note that not everyone is affected the same way. There are such things called protective factors. Protective factors decrease the likelihood that an individual will experience an ACE growing up, and multiple protective factors can build up resilience. In simplest words, resilience can essentially counteract some of the damage done by ACEs.

Protective factors can be done by individual family units or they can be performed by whole communities. The focus of protective factors placed on individual family units is typically on the behavior of the caregiver, which is any adult who is taking care of the child. This can be the biological parents, the adoptive parents, or another blood relative. Examples of protective factors that fall under this category are

- Caregivers who have a steady source of income
- Caregivers who help their children with conflict resolution
- Families that partake in activities together
- Families that provide strong social support.


The community includes things such as academic buildings, government programs, and neighborhoods that are clustered together. Protective factors that are specific to the community include

- Financial programs
- After-school clubs and activities

- Strong relationships between local businesses and the community
- High-quality medical services.

## The Problem of Unresolved Trauma

If you identify any ACE as something that you've experienced throughout your childhood, it is vital that you make the effort to start the healing process. The long-term effects of ACEs are seemingly endless and can affect many different aspects of your life. Your health, your cognitive function, even your social life can be affected by these past events. Unresolved trauma threatens the overall quality of your life, and the longer that it remains unresolved, the longer you have to deal with the unfortunate consequences.

Sometimes, you look back at certain aspects of your life and realize that it all ties back to a few definite moments. You may cringe away from men because your father used to punish you with a wooden spoon. You may have developed an eating disorder because you were deprived of a stable source of food when you were younger. You might have low self-esteem because your mother would berate you and would often put the blame on you for things out of your control. These are all signs that your unresolved trauma has started to make its way into your adulthood. What are other such things that you need to look out for?

# 3

## Body and Brain Effects of Childhood Trauma

*The alarm on her phone began to ring, but Jamie just hit snooze and rolled back over. There was no point in getting up out of bed and getting ready for work. She no longer had a job to get ready for, anyway. Her boss had come over to talk to her about her multiple tardies, and when he caught Jamie sleeping on the job, he fired her on the spot.*

*She tossed herself onto her back and stared at the ceiling. She couldn't fall back asleep. Jamie felt like an utter piece of crap. Jamie felt exhausted. Jamie felt overwhelmed. Jamie felt heartache.*

*Jamie felt nothing.*

*Suddenly, her chest began to feel tighter. She gripped her bedsheets as her breathing quickened. Something is wrong. She is in danger. Jamie is in danger. Her muscles tightened all throughout her body. She should be getting ready for work right now. How could she be stupid enough to make so many mistakes? She should've known better. She can't afford rent now. Her mother will be so disappointed. Her mother will be so disappointed. Her mother will be so disappointed.*

*Tears well up in her eyes. Jamie tries to fight them back, but instead she lets out one massive sob.*

· · · · ● · ● · · ·

Even though the trauma occurs during childhood, it still has troublesome affects all throughout adulthood. Unresolved trauma leads to pain in both the body and the mind, with these ailments nurturing a cyclic nature that cause each other to develop. The only way out is to resolve it and to heal the trauma. When looking for signs that your trauma is making its way into your adult life, you need to look both into your physical health and your mental health.

## Signs to Watch Out For

Major depressive disorder (MDD), otherwise known as depression, is a mood disorder that can appear in individuals who have experienced at least one ACE. MDD is characterized by a loss of energy, a loss of interest in activities that one may have once enjoyed, a change in appetite, a change in sleeping pattern, difficulty concentrating, feelings of depression or sadness, self-harm, and thoughts of suicide. MDD can make it difficult for one to perform daily life skills, such as basic hygiene and being able to feed oneself everyday.

Panic attacks are a symptom of many different mental illnesses, but they don't always mean that you have one. They can also occur in neurotypical individuals when there is an abundance of anxiety happening at one time. Panic attacks are often confused with heart attacks when they are occurring, especially in those who are not familiar with them, as the symptoms are very familiar. It will cause the heartbeat to quicken and it will make it harder to breathe. Oftentimes, hyperventilation will begin. The chest will begin to tighten. Nausea, sweating, and shaking can set in. It is common for the individual experiencing the panic attack to feel as if they are going to die at that moment. Panic attacks typically last anywhere from five minutes to twenty minutes, with the worst of the symptoms occurring in the first ten minutes.

Social anxiety disorder is characterized by the excessive fears and worries surrounding different aspects of social interactions. Panic attacks can often be triggered by forced social interactions such as having to participate in an academic or work setting. Individuals with social anxiety disorder will avoid social interactions, and go to extreme costs to do so. For instance, they can change their daily route going to work if someone is in their way and might possibly interact with them.

There are several different types of eating disorders that one can develop after living through an ACE. In relation to the amount of food that is being allowed into the body, there are four eating disorders in total. There is anorexia nervosa, bulimia nervosa, binge eating disorder, and avoidant restrictive food intake disorder (ARFID).

Anorexia nervosa, otherwise just known as anorexia, is when an individual is living with an intense fear of gaining weight. Because of this fear, the individual partakes in starving themself in order to prevent any weight gain. When food is eaten, it is typically low-calorie foods that are followed by extreme exercise. In those who experience menstrual cycles, anorexia nervosa can cause periods to stop entirely. Bones become fragile and muscles become weak.

Bulimia nervosa, otherwise just known as bulimia, is similar to anorexia nervosa, but includes the act of binge eating and then expelling the food from the body. When the individual is not eating low-calorie foods, there is a chance that they are eating mass amounts of food in a short amount of time. These binges are often associated with feelings of guilt and shame. After a binge, the individual expels the food from the body. This can be done in many ways, such as making oneself vomit, taking a laxative, working off all of the calories, and fasting. If someone with bulimia nervosa is making themself vomit, they could eventually suffer from damage to their tooth enamel due to frequent incidents of stomach acid inside the mouth and dehydration due to the different ways to expel food.

Binge eating disorder is similar to bulimia nervosa in the way that they both have periods of binging large quantities of food, but unlike bulimia, those with binge eating disorder do not have the desire to expel the food from their bodies after consuming it. They also do not participate in fasting or diet culture outside of binging. Individuals with binge eating disorder participate in binging at least once a week.

ARFID is often diagnosed alongside obsessive-compulsive disorder (OCD). It is characterized by either picky eating or the fear that certain foods will hurt the individual in some way if consumed. These two characteristics must be extreme enough to cause the individual to be significantly underweight or have some form of nutritional deficiency.

If you recognize any of the symptoms, behaviors, or situations listed above in any of these health conditions in yourself, or if you have already been diagnosed with one, there is a chance that your experience with an ACE as a child may have affected your health as an adult today.

There are other ways that ACEs can affect your adult self that aren't necessarily health conditions, but still have a major impact on one's health, personal life, and social life. For example, individuals who have lived through at least one ACE have an increased chance of using substances in order to cope with their trauma. This can include alcohol, marijuana, cocaine, and other drugs. Using these substances in order to cope can result in substance abuse and addiction. Each different type of substance used comes with it's own health detriments. There are other types of destructive behaviors that one can use to cope with having gone through an ACE, such as indulging in sex, food, and gambling.

Destructive behaviors can expand into the realm of physical self-harm, such as cutting, burning, or hitting oneself.

Experiencing an ACE can lead to personal issues such as low self-esteem and anxieties over a wide variety of different topics. One of these anxieties is characterized by a concern about whether the people around them are judging them or not. This can stem from emotional abuse one may have experienced during childhood, or it could potentially stem from the reaction of others when the ACE occurred. For instance, when a child comes to school with bruises, there will probably be whispers coming from the other students. This can be perceived as those other children judging the victim of the physical abuse. This fear of judgment can in turn develop into chronic people pleasing, where one individual will do whatever it takes to make others happy. There's another reason why this is done. Someone can partake in chronic people pleasing because they want to make sure that others are happy so that they don't deal with the consequences if they are not. ACEs often occur when a parent or guardian is lashing out at a child, so if they are content, no harm is to be brought forth.

Social issues that one living with the aftereffects of an ACE can experience includes difficulty trusting others. This comes from the fear that someone else will take advantage and hurt them just like they had been hurt in the past. These trust issues transfer into romantic relationships, causing individuals to either jump from relationship to relationship, or to find themselves trusting the wrong types of individuals and ending up in abusive relationships. If marriage does happen, sexual issues, such as an extremely low or high libido, an inability to get aroused, or inability to have an orgasm can occur.

• • • • ● • ● • • • •

*"Come on, Jamie! You always do this to me." Ken climbed out of bed and yanked his pants on.*

*"I'm sorry, I'm so sorry! Baby, please come back into bed. I can finish you off, if you want. Whatever you want, I'll do it." Jamie bundled the comforter up to her chest.*

*"We can't keep doing this. I can't even have sex with my own girlfriend! I'm done. You're too much." He threw his shirt on over his head.*

*"Baby, let me blow you, please. We can just forget about this! I'm sorry I'm not ready. I just can't right now." She stretched out her hand towards Ken. He smacked it away and pointed a finger in her face.*

*"I said I'm done. I'm leaving, you fat piece of crap." He snatched a pack of cigarettes off of the nightstand next to the bed and pulled one out. He then pulled the lighter out of his pants pocket, lighting the single cigarette and bringing it to his lips. "I'll grab my stuff tomorrow. Make sure to have it all ready and packed for me."*

*"Yes Ken," Jamie said. She didn't dare move from the bed. She watched as he made his way out the door of her bedroom. He slammed the door to her apartment.*

*Jamie stared at a blank spot on her wall. A shiver came across her, and she covered herself up with the comforter. She felt exposed. As her mind began to wander about how on earth she was going to pack all of his stuff by tomorrow, she felt 10 sharp pricks as she began to mindlessly dig her nails into her skin. When she became aware that she was doing this, she didn't stop.*

• • • ● • ● • • •

## How to Know if You Need Professional Help

Many of the signs of trauma leaking into adulthood are also aspects of life that can be ultimately unrelated to trauma entirely. Someone with mental illness can possibly have a chemical imbalance, such as a lack of the neurotransmitter serotonin. Eating disorders can be caused by society's view on the way women should look rather than an individual's need for control in their life. Sexual issues can be caused by other health conditions, medications you may be on, or even just your age. If there are so many other factors that come into it, how do you know that these signs are specifically from your trauma? And when is it time for you to get help from a professional?

Some individuals are able to identify on their own that they need to contact a professional. They see that their quality of life has deteriorated in such a way that they can no longer function like they were once able to. This is a red flag for them and they decide to take precautions to ask for outside help.

Unfortunately, not everyone can tell when they need to get help. Sometimes, unhealthy behaviors and conditions become the new normal to the person, so they see no reason to try to change it. In cases like these, people the individual is close to will take notice. This can be friends, family, coworkers, or even neighbors. These people can step in and bring awareness to the suffering individual that they may need help.

When others step in, there can be some pushback. If the individual themself doesn't see the need for help, it can seem as if the people in their life are sticking their noses into their business, or like they don't believe that they can't handle it themself. This isn't true. Outside help is sometimes required in order to get better, and yet, there is a belief among some cultures that getting help means that you are a burden or a failure. When it comes to getting professional help, it can be seen as a weakness, but this is not the case. It is important to note that if people in your life are bringing to your attention that you may need professional help, it is for good reason. These people care for you and want what is best for you. Getting professional help is a huge step in the healing process.

Overall, it doesn't matter where the motivation comes from to get help. What matters is that you gain awareness of the things that you are experiencing. You are experiencing feelings of hurt, loss, and pain. Instead of attempting to push those feelings down or pushing them aside while you focus on other things, try being aware that those are very real emotions that are going on in your body. Your experiences are real, and so are all of the things that you are feeling because of them.

Try gaining awareness of the fact that you are going through at least one ACE that may have created several aftereffects for you as an adult. Know that these adverse effects are not your fault. They are due to the unfortunate circumstances that you had no control over as a child. There is plenty of help out there to assist you with your recovery process. All you have to do is recognize the signs that you need help.

You recognized certain behaviors or certain medical conditions that were listed, but how do you know that you need treatment for unresolved trauma rather than just the behavior or medical condition? Luckily, there are a few things to look out for.

## Signs You Need Help

People who are struggling from unresolved trauma often have their home and work life impacted as well. One may be turning in subpar work at their place of employment. They may be irritable with coworkers or management because they disagree with something that they are doing. It eventually gets to the point where they will begin to come in late or miss work entirely, causing them to get fired from job after job. Home life isn't much better. Activities that were once enjoyable now get put aside either for destructive behaviors or can lead to destructive behaviors. Interpersonal relationships are harder to handle because of trust issues, so support systems can dissolve.

Along with trust issues among interpersonal relationships, people will often feel disconnected from others. It becomes hard to form close bonds that people who haven't experienced an ACE find much easier to do. This can affect even pre-existing bonds that people already have, causing relationships that could have existed for years to start to weaken. This isolates the individual, and they can begin to feel emotionally numb.

Extreme feelings of depression and anxiety can be a sign that it is time to get help. If your depression and anxiety alone are getting in the way of your everyday life to the point where you must adjust several aspects of it, something needs to be done. Excessive amounts of anxiety can trap someone in their own thoughts and essentially prevent them from doing anything because they keep circling in their own self-doubt. Adding depression on top of that takes away their energy to be able to do something when they don't have anxiety. It is a double battle that one must fight in order to just do tasks that others would consider normal or typical of everyday life.

Due to trauma, one can experience flashbacks during the day and nightmares while they are asleep. These bring the person back to unwanted memories of the traumatic events of their past, making them relive it over and over again. These flashbacks and nightmares are completely out of the individual's control, and so they are left helpless whenever they occur. In hopes of avoiding these events, trauma victims tend to avoid anything that could potentially remind them of their past traumas. This could be huge things that are similar to the trauma event, such as the trauma depicted in media, or little things, such as the abuser's favorite snack or perhaps a song that played during a particularly terrifying memory in one's past.

Coping with substances should not occur, and if you are doing so, that is a good indication that it is time to get professional help. Substances, while having the ability to make someone feel good in the short-term, have a long list of negative side effects from short-term and long-term usage. These substances are not permanent solutions to the problem, and do not replace any step in the healing process. Using substances in order to cope only leads to addiction and substance abuse.

• • • • ● • ● • • • •

*Jamie wanted nothing more than to continue eating her gallon of rocky road, but the incessant pounding on the door would not let up. She huffed as she got up. Peeking through the peephole, she saw that it was her friend, Sarah. Well, at least, she still considered Sarah a friend. They didn't exactly have a falling out, but they haven't spoken in a few weeks.*

*Jamie opened the door. "Hey, Sarah. I wasn't expecting company. Otherwise, I would've actually gotten dressed today." She was wearing gray sweatpants, fuzzy socks, and a white tank top with no bra on. Her hair was in a slept-in bun from the night before, and she hadn't brushed her teeth yet.*

*"Hey! You're okay! I heard about Ken. Is it okay if I come in?"*

*Jamie shrugged and gestured inside. As Sarah entered the apartment, Jamie rushed to put away her leftover ice cream. It would have to wait awhile.*

*"Do you need anything? Like a glass of water or something?" Jamie asked as she sat down in her armchair. Sarah was already sitting on the couch next to it.*

*She turned her body toward Jamie. "No, no! I'm alright." She grabbed Jamie's hands softly, rubbing her thumbs against the back of them. "I'm not gonna be by for long. I just wanted to check up on you. You've got a bad luck streak going on, and I really care about you."*

*Jamie adjusted in her seat. "I mean, it's no big deal, really. Ken wasn't great for me anyway, and I'm going to find a new job, and AA meetings have been going really great so far."*

*Sarah stared at her for a moment. Jamie looked away, toward the floor.*

*"Can I be really honest with you and have you not get mad at me?"*

*Jamie matched Sarah's eyes once more. "Sarah, I've known you for years. Of course."*

*"I'm worried about you. Like, legitimately worried about you. I think it might be time that you seek help other than AA." Sarah squeezed Jamie's hands.*

*Jamie sighed and paused for a moment.*

*"I think you're right.*

· · · · ● · ● · · ·

If you've identified anything that has been in this chapter within yourself, it may be time to take action. In this next chapter, we will discuss different therapy modalities that one can look into when starting their journey with professional help.

# 4

## THERAPY FOR HEALING FROM CHILDHOOD TRAUMA

*"So what do I even look up? I don't even know where to start," Jamie asked.*

*"I mean, I've got a few suggestions on where to start, but ultimately, it's completely up to you," Sarah replied. "I've got a great therapist that specializes in cognitive behavioral therapy, if you're interested in that. I can give you her contact information."*

*Jamie hesitated before answering. "I'm not sure. It's just talk therapy, right? What if I need a lot more than that? You know my parents."*

*"I wouldn't doubt the power of talk therapy if I were you. My therapist has been able to get me through a lot, you know. I feel a lot better as a person ever since I started going."*

*Jamie started to pick at the skin on her thumb. "What if it's not enough, though? I'm 37 and I'm still dealing with this. I can't even hold a job!"*

*Sarah reached over and grabbed Jamie's hands once again, stopping her from picking at her thumbs. "We're going to keep working at it until we find something that works for you, okay? There are plenty of different options out there. You don't know how you're going to react to them until you actually get out there and start trying them. So let's get out there and do exactly that."*

* * * * * * * * * * *

There is a huge stigma around the idea that those who go to therapy are weaker than those who don't. This stigma needs to be removed because it is absolutely not true. In many cases, therapy is necessary for the healing process to commence. Therefore, you should feel safe enough to reach out for the help that you both need and deserve. Mental health services should be given the same respect that physical health services are given so that individuals who need that help are unafraid of receiving it. That is not to mention that trauma is both a mental and physical ailment and should be treated as such in terms of recovery. As you go through your healing process, constant affirmations that you are not weak for reaching out for professional mental health services are a must.

## Hotlines for Immediate Assistance

While being able to go to therapy for recovery is necessary, there are situations in which you simply cannot wait long enough to get the help you need in therapy. If you feel like you are going to self-harm or otherwise seriously harm yourself or others, you need to reach out in that exact moment. The same applies if your living situation is harmful to your well-being. This could mean that you are currently living with or you are in frequent contact with someone who emotionally, physically, or sexually abuses you. Waiting for your next therapy appointment could be too late. For immediate assistance, there are several hotline numbers that one can contact. These include

- Calling 800-273-8255 to reach the National Suicide Prevention Lifeline
- Calling 800-950-6264 to reach the National Alliance on Mental Illness
- Calling 800-799-72333 or texting START to 88788 to reach the National Domestic Violence Hotline
- Texting HOME to 741741 to reach the Crisis Text Line

Each of the lines have their own valuable role to play in a crisis situation. The National Suicide Prevention Lifeline helps individuals who are feeling suicidal at the time of calling and will give free confidential support to those in the United States. The National Alliance on Mental Illness can provide guidance on a person's next steps on their mental health journey and support those who are affected by mental illness. This can include someone who has a mental illness diagnosis, or someone who is trying to help somebody else that does. The National Domestic Violence Hotline offers crisis intervention and referral services for those who are experiencing domestic abuse in their life. The Crisis Text Line is used for crisis intervention and to provide support for mental health based emergencies.

Outside of what is designed for emergency situations, let's look into the different therapy modalities and see which one is right for you.

## Low-Cost Assistance

If you're worried about the high-cost that is typically associated with mental health services, there are plenty of options out there for you. Taking care of your mental health doesn't have to be expensive. If you have health insurance, investigate what services are covered under your plan. You can call local mental health services in your area that take your health insurance to see if they can tell you approximately how much their services will cost. If you don't currently have health insurance and live in the United States, see if you qualify for Medicaid or Medicare. Many people with either of these two types of health insurances can receive mental health services entirely for free.

Some private clinics who do not take health insurance offer a sliding scale for their costs. If you are willing to see a therapist in training, then you will be able to pay a much lower cost compared to what you would've had to pay seeing an already fully trained therapist. Along these lines, there are many locations that have students attempting to train to become fully licensed therapists outside of private clinics. These include university hospitals or training institutes. Receiving therapy at these places can cost little to nothing, and are definitely worth looking into.

## Available Therapy Approaches

So many types of therapy have been developed since the invention of clinical psychology in 1896. Therapy is not just limited to talk therapy, as many believe when they hear the word. There are types of therapy that can teach people how to control certain physiological responses in order to relax their body during distress, there are therapies that override traumatic memories, and there are therapies that evaluate where you are with different aspects of your life. If one style doesn't particularly work for you, there are several more options that you can try out instead.

Each therapy varies in how it approaches healing, price ranges, how widespread availability is, and how long the average person stays in the therapy. Finding an institution that does a form of talk therapy in your area might be easier than finding one that performs neurofeedback, but that does not mean that neurofeedback will not be worth it to you. Instead of just settling for the type of therapy that is closest to you, the cheapest, and the shortest, try weighing out the pros and cons for each type of therapy for your specific situation. You don't want to rule out anything simply because you believe it is out of your reach. You deserve the chance to get to heal, even if that means you have to do a bit of research beforehand to see what you may like. We can at least get some of that research covered right here as a starting point.

### Eye Movement Desensitization and Reprocessing (EMDR)

Eye Movement Desensitization and Reprocessing (EMDR) therapy is designed to help process memories and attach positive emotions to the events that occur within the memories rather than the negative emotions that pre-exist in them. This is accomplished by putting the brain in the same mode that it is put in when it goes to sleep. During sleep, the brain processes through memories and solidifies them. This is when memories get moved from short-term memory to long-term memory. In EMDR, while the brain is in this state, one can change how the traumatic memory is written.

How does this process work? How can the brain get put into a sleeplike state without actually being asleep? It's a lot simpler than one would believe. All that has to be done is have the client track the therapist's finger with their eyes, and then the brain is suddenly using the same processes that it uses during sleep. While doing this, the client focuses on one aspect of their trauma and then attempts to clear their mind. After the memory brings no distress, they will repeat the measures, but with a positive belief, such as that the client came out stronger for having gone through what they did.

**Individual Psychotherapy**

Psychotherapy is the traditional form of the therapy that we think of when we think of therapy. Unlike the other forms of therapy that are in this chapter, psychotherapy tends to be used directly to help those diagnosed with mental illnesses, although those who have not been diagnosed are also free to use them.

There are four types of psychotherapy to date: psychodynamic, humanistic, behavioral, and cognitive. The exact purpose of psychotherapy depends on the type of psychotherapy that is being performed. In order of the list above, the purposes of psychotherapies are to determine any possible causes of pain, to promote self-growth, to alleviate the physical symptoms of mental illness, and to teach coping mechanisms for mental symptoms.

Since each type of psychotherapy has a different purpose, make sure to look into the different types before going into psychotherapy. If you are suffering from low self-esteem, try looking into humanistic psychotherapies in your area. If you are struggling with having unclear memories of your past, try looking into psychodynamic psychotherapies in your area.

Many therapists who perform psychotherapy combine different types in order to give their clients a more rounded experience. Some therapists, like behavioral therapists, will outright state the type of therapy practices they use before you even ask. Others have no problem going into detail if you do ask them, so don't be afraid to call before making an appointment to make sure that a therapist in the area is right for you.

## Cognitive Behavioral Therapy

*Jamie took a big breath, held it in, and finally released it. "I'll give it a try, but you have to promise me that you're going to be by my side. I feel nauseous just looking at all of this."*

*Sarah offered a smile and a nod. Jamie brought her attention back to her phone. Where to start? She typed in "therapist near me" in the tab pulled up on her phone. Pages upon pages of Google search results popped up. Jamie bit her lip as she scrolled through. Her eyes landed on one page in particular.*

*"What about this one? Dr. Clarke? She looks friendly enough."*

*Sarah nodded. "Let's schedule an appointment."*

Cognitive behavioral therapy (CBT) is a type of individual psychotherapy. It falls under the type of cognitive psychotherapy, but also uses some principles from behavioral psychotherapy as well. CBT focuses on teaching individuals how to change thoughts and behaviors that are harmful to their well-being. It takes a look at the current situation and how it can be fixed, as events in the past are set in stone.

In a typical session of CBT, you will be taught how to recognize harmful thoughts and behaviors in yourself. From there, the therapist helps replace those harmful actions with more beneficial ones, or at the very least, ones that make sense with the situation. For instance, if someone is having trouble bringing a concern up to a friend because they are afraid their friend is going to hate them for it, then the therapist can teach the individual how to view the scenario more logically. Rather than hate them, their friend is more likely to take the criticism calmly and to listen to them.

CBT typically requires clients to have homework, where clients have to practice the things they learned in therapy at home. While this further solidifies the skills you learn in CBT, it can be a huge time commitment. Due to this, everyone may not have the time to dedicate to CBT.

## Cognitive Processing Therapy

Further categorizing the types of psychotherapies, cognitive processing therapy (CPT) is a subset of CBT specifically designed to help those diagnosed with post-traumatic stress disorder (PTSD).

Much like in CBT, CPT aims to change harmful thoughts, except CPT focuses on thoughts related to trauma. At the start of the first session, the client is told to write a statement on how the trauma they've experienced has impacted them. Then, the client picks a traumatic experience and writes about it in as much detail as they can provide. With the therapist, the client will go over the experience and try to pick out any harmful thoughts and the feelings that are associated with the event. The therapist will work with the client from there to identify coping mechanisms that can help the client when those harmful thoughts come back into play. This gives power back to the individual living with PTSD.

Unlike some forms of psychotherapy, CPT can be both an individual and a group therapy, depending on what the client is looking for. If you are interested in a group setting, a CPT therapist would be able to give you the information you need, and a referral to any sessions you are looking for. If the idea of group therapy sounds uncomfortable or even stressful, there is nothing wrong with just sticking to individual CPT.

## Biofeedback

Biofeedback is a therapy that teaches individuals how to be aware of how their body reacts to stress. With mindfulness of how your body reacts, the end goal of biofeedback is to allow you to ultimately be able to control your body processes so you can better calm your physiological responses in moments of distress. Controlling body temperature, heart rate, and muscle tension are the main focuses.

The average biofeedback therapy session is 30 to 60 minutes long. During this time, a therapist will measure how your body reacts to certain situations using electrical sensors. After they have collected the measurements, the therapist will then go over with you various relaxation techniques that are designed specifically to help you, based on your measurements. The therapist will make sure you thoroughly know a technique and can properly relax your body before moving on to another technique.

Due to the way that biofeedback therapy is set up, it is thought to be more of a training process rather than a treatment. However, this debate over what exactly it should be called doesn't change the therapeutic aftereffects that it has.

## Neurofeedback

Neurofeedback is a specific type of biofeedback otherwise known as electroencephalogram biofeedback. This type of biofeedback focuses on brain activity rather than the other physiological functions that biofeedback as a whole looks at.

In neurofeedback, electrical sensors are placed on the individual's scalp while they play a video game. When the electrical sensors detect brain waves associated with calmness, nothing happens. When the electrical sensors detect a brain wave associated with something such as distraction or distress, it stops the game. This encourages the user to only have calm emotions, so they may continue playing the game.

In addition to training the individual, neurofeedback has recently shown potential in being able to perform structural changes in the brain. In other words, neurofeedback might be able to reverse some of the physical effects adverse childhood events have on the brain. However, before settling on anything just yet, more research is needed in this specific area to confirm or deny this theory.

## Meditation and Mindfulness Training

Meditation and mindfulness exercises are a proven way to alleviate many of the various symptoms of PTSD (Shaw, 2021). They increase bodily awareness of certain functions, such as your breathing and any sensations that are going on throughout your body.

With meditation and mindfulness training, honing one's attentive abilities is key. An increase in attention skills allows for individuals to better ground themselves when they are experiencing moments of stress and anxiety. This particular treatment is great because you are in complete control of what you want your specific practice to look like. If you want, you can reach out to get advice from a mental health professional, but it is not required for your practice. There are also several phone apps available that can guide you through different meditations if you don't want to do it completely by yourself.

While meditation and mindfulness training is great in reducing PTSD symptoms, it is not an advised treatment to be used by itself. Meditation and mindfulness is not sufficient on its own, and will require the use of another therapy to help support it.

## Relational-Cultural Therapy

This type of therapy views the relationships that people hold as the key to our mental well-being. When something is wrong with our relationships, we become mentally unbalanced. Oftentimes, this feeling of something being wrong stems from isolation. This isolation doesn't necessarily have to be when we are literally alone. Isolation also arises when we are in conflict in one or more of our relationships. For example, if someone got into a bad argument with a friend over some money that was owed, and the two were not on speaking terms, that would be a conflict in the relationship.

Relational-cultural therapy works to improve an individual's interdependence, which helps with people who are living with trust issues. When going in for relational-cultural therapy, you would go in for one-on-one sessions with just you and the therapist. Typically, you will go through a large amount of sessions, depending on what you and the therapist discuss as necessary. There are options to do a smaller number of sessions and group therapy, but these versions have a specific manual for the therapist to use, so you may not feel like you are getting a personalized experience. During therapy, you will be taught interpersonal skills and resilience.

**Personal Wellness Card Sort: Help People See Their Strengths**

The personal wellness card sort is an activity that can be done in relational-cultural therapy. In this activity, the therapist brings in cards that list different self-care activities and aspects of life that one needs to feel whole. Examples of self-care activities include exercise and friendships. Cultural identity and control are examples of aspects of life one needs to feel whole.

The individual who is attending therapy then has to sort the cards by which ones they feel like they have a great handle on in life, which ones they feel like they have covered, and which ones they need to work more on. They will go over with the therapist why they put each card in the category that they did, and they will have the opportunity to move any card after talking it out.

Then, the therapist and client focus on how they can move the cards that need to be worked on in a pile that feels more stable in the client's life. Which cards are within the client's control, and which ones aren't? For the ones that are in their control, the therapist and client can make a plan on how to move the card to a more satisfactory part of life. For example, if the client puts the card "nutrition" in with the cards that need more work, they can make a plan about changing their diet.

For the cards that are out of the client's control, they are more likely than not cards that relate to interpersonal relationships, in which the therapist will take the time to work on interpersonal skills with the client.

If you're curious about the personal wellness card sort, or any of the other therapies mentioned, keep reading on to see how emotions are processed from a traumatic event.

# 5

## WHY THERAPY WORKS

*"My mother always expected more from me than what I could actually offer.
And my father, to him I was nonexistent to the point of starvation."*

*Silence filled the room between Jamie and Dr. Clarke. Dr. Clarke looked
at Jamie with sympathetic eyes, but didn't dare speak just yet. Jamie felt
something bubbling inside of her. It felt uncomfortable, and it wanted out.*

*She looked at the ground. "I was just a kid. I was just a freaking kid. They
were supposed to make me feel safe and sound. Instead, they left me hungry
and hurt. How can you do that to a kid?" Her eyes started to get blurry. She
didn't realize that she had started crying. "I'm angry all the time, Dr. Clarke.
I hate that about myself. I'm angry that they did that to me and I'm scared
it's going to happen again."*

*Dr. Clarke nodded along and handed Jamie a box of tissues. "I see. Take your
time processing what you're feeling. It can be a lot to handle. I want you to
know that while you're here, we are going to work on skills so you don't feel
like those events are going to happen again."*

· · · · ● · ● · · · ·

Processing through emotions can be a difficult experience for some
people, and honestly a bit nerve-racking. Sometimes, individuals can
relive memories from their trauma while processing the events that
had happened. It is recommended that you seek professional help as
you start this process, as it can be hard to get through. Try to work

with smaller memories first and then build up to processing larger trauma events that have happened in your past. This will make it less overwhelming for you.

Although difficult, processing through your emotions is a necessary part of healing, and a rewarding one at that. What exactly does the process look like?

## The Process

In general, there are many ways someone can process their emotions. Some people use only one way to process what it is that they're going through, while others use multiple. Some individuals heal a lot quicker than others. What your unique recovery process looks like compared to others shouldn't matter. It's yours—and not theirs—for a reason.

There are 11 different steps to processing emotions. It's a good idea to try out several of them to see which ones give you the most benefit, even if you think that you found the perfect step from the start. Each memory you process could require a different method in order to work through it. That's another reason why you may want to seek professional help before beginning this process. They can help guide you as you try to find your way on your journey. Which steps are right for you?

### Feel Your Feelings

Rather than trying to push away your negative emotions related to your traumatic experience, try openly expressing them in a safe, controlled environment. Keeping emotions bottled up actively works against any progress you've made toward processing your emotions.

Being able to feel your emotions freely allows for you to have the chance to distinguish what exactly you are feeling because of it. Simply put, feeling sad is the best indicator that we feel sad about a certain event. When everything is kept back, it is harder to distinguish between all of the emotions that a particular event has triggered within you. It all becomes blurred together and the only thing you associate with it is negativity. With emotions that are indistinguishable like that, you cannot give them the individual attention and care that they need, as every emotion needs something different to remedy it.

It is best to do this step in an environment that you feel safe in. Not only will you be experiencing some negative emotions, you will not be sure of the specifics of those negative emotions. Assure that you are with someone who you trust and who is prepared for the situation to come.

## Grounding

In a whirlwind of emotions, it can be easy to feel disconnected from the situation entirely. Many feel overwhelmed and stressed from not being able to put a name to each separate emotion that they are feeling. If you find yourself relating to this, grounding might be helpful to you. In this step, meditation and mindfulness exercises are used in order to bring awareness to the body. Do a cycle of relaxing your muscles and then tightening them, taking notice of how your body feels between each shift.

This is a really great way to calm yourself down before you begin to process emotions. Going into a potentially stressful part of the recovery process while you are already feeling overwhelmed is only going to make the situation worse for you. It could even prevent you from making any progress at all, as you won't know for certain what negative emotion is coming from the trauma and what is coming from outside stress. Going into the healing process with a positive mindset is your best chance for a positive outcome.

## Recall

Most often, a memory of the event can trigger your emotions. If you choose to do this step, once again, make sure that you are in a safe and controlled environment. Have a self-care activity nearby to do right after this step, as it can be distressing.

Try to remember a trauma event you experienced. Start off with something small so that it will not bring you too much distress afterward. Use all five of your senses in doing so to get the full effect of the event. Take note of the emotions that the event makes you feel, and what parts of the event cause different emotions.

If at any point during this step you feel uncomfortable, distressed, or panicked, it is important to stop. You are not weak for not being able to live through a painful memory. Everyone has different tolerances when it comes to their trauma. Some individuals are able to freely talk about their experiences a short period of time after something occurred to them, while others may need years to process the events that have happened. Everyone recovers at their own pace. Self-care is the most important thing if you do not start to feel well after recalling a memory.

**Sense**

This step goes along very well with the step of grounding and has the same purpose. They both are used to calm the individual down when they feel overwhelmed and stressed.

During your meditation, scan your body, starting at the top of the head and going down to the tip of your toes. Pause the scan whenever you notice a sensation going on in your body, and dwell on it. Is that sensation an ache, a pain, a breeze blowing on your skin? Maybe you become aware of the clothes you are wearing. Perhaps you slept in an uncomfortable position that night before, and now your neck hurts a bit. Try to take note of all of these little things we tune out in our everyday lives. Don't be harsh on yourself if you find your mind wandering to other things. Just be gentle in bringing yourself back to the task at hand.

After you've done a full body scan, do the same, but with your environment. What are the different things that you can taste, see, feel, smell, and hear around you? The experience of scanning your environment will be vastly different depending on where you are, so if you feel like you need more time after completing your scan, try moving to a different location to do another scan.

**Name**

It can be simply overwhelming feeling the emotions that you have. However, once you start to feel them, you should be able to differentiate between the many emotions that you may be having. Most of the time, tears mean sadness, wanting to hit something means anger, and feeling your body shake means fear.

Not every emotion fits in one of these perfect boxes, though. Sometimes, they overlap. The presence of tears can occur during an overfill of any emotion, so you can cry when you are happy, angry, or frustrated, not just when you are sad. Wanting to hit something can also come from excitability, where a person has too much energy and nowhere to put it.

If you're having trouble putting names to the emotions that you're feeling, try comparing them to other times you've felt similar emotions. You think you might recognize this as anger, so has this experience felt like another time you've felt anger before? It could help to write down the experiences of the emotions that you're feeling. Then, you could use that in order to identify your emotions. For instance, if you write down that you were shaking, breathing heavily, and your eyes kept darting around the room, it is safe to assume that you were feeling frightened.

**Acceptance**

One reason we tend to bottle up our negative emotions is because we do not believe that we are entitled to them. We make this requirement for ourselves that we must always present ourselves as happy to others, even when we are not. This, in turn, affects how we express emotion when we are alone and when we are with people who we trust.

Instead of allowing ourselves negative emotions toward a situation, we try to skip right to the part where we feel like we have grown from our experience or that we have become stronger because of it. While yes, it is good to eventually get to that point of positivity, you are allowed to take a few stops before getting there. You are entitled to any emotions that you may have resulting from your traumatic experiences. It is not wrong to feel the way that you do. Accept the fact that these negative emotions are a part of your healing process, and you can even come to love that part of yourself. You deserve to be angry, sad, frightened, and every emotion in between.

## Experience

During your time experiencing your emotions, make sure that you are fully present. Acknowledge your feelings, even welcome them into your body. Fully embrace the discomforts that they bring. As necessary as they are, does anyone actually like experiencing negative emotions? Possibly not, but both your body and mind will feel much better once everything has been released.

Express your emotions in a productive way. It is okay to cry or scream into a pillow, but stay away from destructive behaviors. Such behaviors will only inhibit the healing process and will actually numb your emotions in most instances. Your emotions need to be acted out, but luckily, they won't last long. When attempting to experience them, make sure that you are in a safe, controlled environment with someone that you trust. Have some self-care activities on standby for when you need to get away from the discomfort. Try to remember that it is okay to go at your own pace while doing this, especially if you are used to pushing such feelings aside. Doing a little at a time rather than doing all at once is recommended. Otherwise, you may feel overwhelmed and become increasingly stressed.

## Listen

Every emotion that you feel occurs for a reason. While you lean into them, try listening in to what they have to say about the situation. You may find out things about yourself that you didn't know previously, or that you refused to learn about yourself. For example, if you find yourself continuously experiencing anger, frustration, or the need to shy away when others compliment your appearance, you may feel ridiculous for experiencing such emotions in reaction to a positive interaction. Being complimented on one's appearance should bring forth feelings of happiness. However, upon leaning into the negative emotions, you may discover that you feel this way because when you were younger, every time your dad complimented your appearance, it was actually a backhanded compliment. As these backhanded compliments were not that common and they were not the forefront of your trauma, you had almost forgotten about them entirely.

Through listening to what your emotions have to say about certain situations, you can gain insight on what things you need to work on, and how specifically you should work on them. Working through an event that has sparked an anger response in you requires different steps than when you are working through an event that has sparked a fear response.

**Journal**

You will hear journaling be recommended to you from almost any therapist that you go to. It's a great way to talk out what it is you're feeling without having to hold a conversation with another person. Writing down your emotions is a better way of processing them than just simply thinking them through because of a few reasons.

For one, writing down what you're feeling allows for a steady stream of consciousness. If you're only thinking about it, it is easy to get distracted and to stray from the original prompt.

Another reason is that writing slows down your thought process. One can become too caught up in their thoughts and can quickly spiral, initiating a panic attack. Writing ensures clearer thoughts and lessens the chance of distress when processing emotions.

The last reason is that with thoughts, you can never go back and look at previous things that you have said. If you believe that you made a breakthrough, unless you have it down in writing, you cannot accurately share it with others if you wanted to later on.

If you want to try journaling, do it in an environment free of distractions for at least 10 minutes every day. Set a timer and just write everything that comes to mind, and don't stop writing until you hear the timer go off.

**Share It**

If you feel comfortable with it, share your emotions! This can be done both figuratively and literally. How does an individual share their emotions figuratively versus literally?

When you share them figuratively, you could write them out in a letter that you don't actually plan on sending. Write the letter to the toxic parent who participated in the ACE or ACEs you experienced, and explain to them your feelings. Let out everything you've been holding back over the years, from childhood up until your current adult life.

When you share them literally, you could find a consenting friend or family member, or a therapist to express your feelings to. If you do this with a friend or family member, it is important to set up boundaries beforehand, as they are not mental health professionals. Let them know if you want them to just listen or if you would rather this be a conversation. If you are speaking to a therapist, there may be some boundaries, but because they are mental health professionals, the conversation would look different than the ones you may create with those you have personal relationships with. For instance, someone you know personally is not required to call the police if you tell them of a current case of child abuse, while a therapist is required. Keep this in mind when you consider sharing your emotions with others.

**Release**

Releasing is a great step that goes along with many of the other steps. It is essentially a way of symbolically letting go of negative emotions tied to traumatic events. This step can be performed right after some of the other steps once you are comfortable with the place you are at, and can look like many various things. Let's look at some examples.

After performing the grounding or sense step, you can visualize the negative emotions as the tightness in your muscles. As you relax, picture your body expelling the negativity. Repeat this cycle with deep breaths until you are completely calm, with each tension release and each exhale, a little more negative emotion escaping your body.

After performing the journaling step, you can tear out the pages you wrote on and dispose of them. This can be done by throwing them away, or by doing something more extravagant, such as burning the paper, shredding it, or tying it to something and throwing it in a body of water.

Similar to the release after the journaling step, if you decided to share your feelings by writing a letter, you can dispose of the letter as a way of stating that you are casting away that part of your life.

No matter the way that you decide to release the negative emotion, the important part is that you release it somehow in a way that you are comfortable with and in a way that feels gratifying to you. You may repeat this process as many times as you like to expel negative emotions and negative energy from your body.

## Trust the Process

This entire process can be uncomfortable at first, but in doing the hard work and in releasing the trauma, the space it took up can begin to be filled with positive energy.

• • • ● • ● • • •

*"You said in our last session that your mother had high expectations of you. Expectations that were too high for a child. Do you mind elaborating on that?" Dr. Clarke asked.*

*Jamie took a second before responding. There were a million moments that all blended together. Her mother's scowl remained the same throughout the years. One specific moment in time stood out to her as she skimmed her memory bank.*

*"There was one time when I was really little where I wanted to play with some little glass fish she had. I thought they were the prettiest thing in the world. Well, something ended up startling me and I broke one. It was a complete accident. Mother was furious. I was banned from entering the same room*

*that held the rest of her fish from that moment on. I just wanted to make her happy, but it was impossible. Kids make mistakes, and she never seemed to understand that."*

*Dr. Clarke wrote something on her notepad. "Do you think the impossible standards your mother set for you as a child could have influenced your need to make sure people are happy today, even if it costs your own happiness?"*

*Silence. "I think so, Dr. Clarke."*

# 6

## AVOIDANCE BEHAVIOR

*It is two months after Jamie moved out of her mother's house. She is 18 years old. She is with her friend Jeremy, who is several years older than her.*

*"I still can't believe a girl like you doesn't drink," he laughs, settling down on the couch next to her, beer in hand. His knee touches her. "If I lived your life, I probably would have drank myself to death by now!"*

*Jamie laughs. "It's just not my thing."*

*Jeremy tilts his bottle toward her. "I think it should be your thing. It'll help you relax. I know how nervous you get sometimes. Trust me, a couple drinks whenever you feel like crap, and you're good as new. Plus, girls who drink are pretty cute."*

*She met his eyes. "You think so?" Instead of replying, he motioned the bottle again toward her. She took it and welcomed her first, and certainly not her last, sip of alcohol.*

· · · · ● · ● · · ·

There's a popular trope in television shows and movies, where one character goes through an incredibly tough breakup, and then proceeds to use casual sex to cope with said breakup. In some cases, the life-changing breakup occurred before the show or movie even began, making the casual sex a defining characteristic for the character. In some cases, this use of casual sex is never resolved, while in others, it is only resolved once the character finds love again.

Practically everyone can name a character that follows this trope. If you expand this trope past bad breakups to the use of casual sex for coping with anything in general, then it's virtually impossible to be unfamiliar with a character who aligns with this trope.

Unfortunately, this is much more than a trope. Casual sex in order to cope with an underlying problem is known as a destructive coping behavior. It's a common numbing behavior, and because it isn't associated with substance abuse, it is often overlooked. People view this use of casual sex as the coping individual just getting back into the dating scene, or they've always been a bit of a player, when in reality, they're trying to avoid the problem at hand.

Casual sex isn't the only type of destructive coping behavior. There are several other types, most of which are more common than one would think. Before we get into the different behaviors we catch ourselves doing, we must ask: What exactly is a destructive coping behavior, and why should it be avoided?

## Destructive Coping Behaviors

Coping behaviors, otherwise known as coping mechanisms, are behaviors that are performed in hopes of increasing one's ability to manage their mental health. This can include managing stress, mental illness symptoms, or PTSD flashbacks. While the intent behind coping behaviors is positive, the lasting effects of them aren't always. Some coping behaviors leave negative impacts on people, and can actually prevent the person from making positive progress toward healing. Destructive coping behaviors can even end up making someone's situation worse by introducing risky behaviors. These risky behaviors may lead to traumatic events such as sexual abuse, physical abuse, addiction, overdose, and self-injury.

These behaviors can be either self-taught or learned from other individuals who are also using them to cope at the same time. When it is self-taught, the individual can partake in the coping behavior for a different reason, such as for recreational purposes, and then realize that the behavior dulls the pain of the traumatic event. This encourages the person to continue to use this coping behavior without learning genuine coping behaviors that would have a positive impact on their healing. When they learn it from someone else, they may confide in that person that they are struggling. That person then might offer the destructive coping behavior as a solution, becoming the guide on how to do the coping behavior, and the partner to do the coping behavior with.

Since destructive coping behaviors often allow for the person using them to seemingly avoid the traumatic event they are trying to cope with, it can be hard to break away from these behaviors. Positive coping behaviors require interaction with the traumatic event, so it is much easier to continue using destructive coping behaviors. Easier does not mean better, though. Unfortunately, because these coping behaviors are easier to fall into, it is harder to transition to positive coping behaviors, and it's easier to fall out of positive coping behaviors. It's important to be able to identify destructive coping behaviors so that you can quickly get out of those situations if you ever find yourself in them.

Now that you know what destructive coping behaviors are in general, what are specific types of these behaviors to look out for?

**Numbing and Avoidance**

Coping behaviors that fall under this category are behaviors that are used to block out the traumatic event and any pain that was caused because of it. This can be changing the actual chemicals inside your brain temporarily so that you are forced to feel a certain emotion, such as using a substance, or it can be doing an activity that makes the participant occupied and feel good in the moment, such as casual sex.

These behaviors are negative for several reasons. For one, they never allow for the healing process to begin, as the trauma is never addressed. Bottled up emotions do not resolve themselves. Instead, they pile up and become worse over time. Your need to partake in numbing and avoidance behaviors may increase, creating a dangerous cycle.

A second reason is that because you never actually get to heal from your trauma using these coping behaviors, you will have to use them every single time you want to escape. Since the recovery process is not in motion, there is no telling how frequently you will have to indulge in these coping behaviors. They also vary in how long they block out the trauma event, so some behaviors will have to be performed more frequently than others.

A third reason is due to the frequency of the coping behavior. Destructive coping behaviors have negative consequences when they are performed. With something such as destructive coping behaviors, where they need to be performed at high frequencies, the negative consequences will increase and stack onto each other. The chances of getting certain negative consequences will also increase as you continue using destructive coping behaviors rather than positive ones.

To put it into perspective, let's look at a few examples of numbing and avoidance coping behaviors. If someone is trying to alleviate the symptom of PTSD flashbacks, they might begin to partake in substance use. More specifically, their cousin has introduced them to heroin. Heroin would be an example of a numbing behavior, as it produces a euphoric feeling that would cancel out any anxiety caused by PTSD flashbacks. However, this individual would get the negative short-term effects of heroin use, such as nausea, dry mouth, and drowsiness. Eventually, the numbing effect of heroin would dissipate, causing the individual to want to use the substance again when the next flashback occurs. For every time that they use, their chances of addiction increases and they start gaining the negative long-term effects, such as brain damage. Once addiction occurs, it's hard to stop because of withdrawal symptoms. As a result, this user will have a difficult time breaking out of their addiction.

Another example is someone using casual sex in order to cope with their major depressive disorder. Sex makes them feel good temporarily, so they participate in it as often as they can. They often meet up with strangers through dating apps. However, because the feel good rush after a meet up doesn't last very long, they have to keep going out in order to cope with their mental illness. Since they go out so frequently with strangers, they have an increased chance of getting a sexually transmitted infection (STI) or causing an accidental pregnancy.

**Blame Game**

Oftentimes with ACEs, children are left without knowing why an event happened to them. When they grow up into adults, this mystery is still left unanswered in many cases. This can cause frustration, especially when we view the world as a place where bad things happen to bad people and good things happen to good people. In reaction, we tend to play the *blame game*, which is where we try to make sense of an event by putting the blame of it on someone or something specific. The blame can be placed on the person who did the traumatic event to you, someone or something who you see filled a protective role in your life, or even yourself. As long as it can create some sort of explanation for why the events that happened during your childhood occurred, then anyone can be put to blame.

While this particular coping behavior can put one at ease, it is still a destructive coping behavior because it does not work toward recovery at all. It only encourages feelings such as anger if the blame is placed on someone else and guilt and shame if the blame is put on yourself. Embracing negative emotions about the ACEs you have experienced is a step toward the recovery process, but there are a few things wrong with going about that in the way of the blame game.

The blame game redirects the negative emotions that you were originally feeling toward the blame that you have placed. This leaves the original feelings untouched and unprocessed. As a result, the effect is the same as that of the numbing and avoidant behaviors, where feelings are left to be bottled up. Except in place of feeling numb in relation to the traumatic event, you feel actively angry or sad about it for a different reason.

You may be thinking to yourself that at least the blame game allows for one to process and to identify their negative emotions, even if it is now to a different scenario than what it was originally. Wasn't that a part of the recovery process, being able to identify your negative emotions and feel through them? Yes, it is, but there's a vital next step that the blame game is missing out on. At some point, you need to be able to move on from those negative emotions that you have processed, and the blame game does not allow for that. All it does is harbor those negative feelings and lets them fester inside of you.

While it only seems natural to try to find a reason for the horrible things that may have happened to you in the past, unfortunately, there isn't always a reason. So many factors can come into play that the blame game just isn't a viable option. When you're having trouble coming to terms with the idea that sometimes, things just happen, try to remember that the world isn't set up where bad things happen only to bad people. You are not a bad person because you had a bad thing happen to you.

## Isolating Yourself

Events such as ACEs aren't widely explored as commonly as other traumatic experiences are in the media. Why is this? It could be due to the fact that seeing children suffer makes adults incredibly uncomfortable, so they would rather see the pain be brought forth onto adults. It could be that media producers are afraid children will see it and their parents will have to explain that bad things can happen to them. No matter the reason, there tends to be a lack of education in terms of ACEs. Since children are not always taught about ACEs, and when they are, they are not taught to a full extent, they do not know what is happening to them if they experience one. This increases the chance of them isolating themselves because they feel like they are the only ones to have experienced the thing they have. As the impacts of one or more ACE come into adulthood, so does the habit of isolating oneself.

Isolation prevents the individual from seeking help, either from their personal relationships or from mental health professionals. It can also inhibit having people from their personal relationships make an effort to reach out because they view the person as just shy, or "they've always been quiet." Without proper representation and education, people will believe that they are alone in their situation and will treat themselves as such. However, they are not alone in the slightest.

Besides representation in media and education on the subject, the best help one can get if they are partaking in isolation as their coping behavior is joining a support group. This solution may not come easily to them, as they think that they are the only one going through what they are going through, but let this be a sign. Keep an open eye on yourself and the ones you love to see signs of isolation from experiencing a traumatic event. A support group, or even group therapy that is focused on a specific topic, will allow for the isolated person to recognize that there are actually many people going through similar situations. They can find support systems in people they would have never thought of going to before, and people who will make them feel like they're not alone in the world.

· • • ●•● • • ·

*"Hello everyone. I'm Jamie."*

*A chorus of 'Hello Jamie' followed suit.*

*"This is my first Alcoholics Anonymous meeting, so I'm not really sure what I'm supposed to say here, but uh, I'm already three days sober. I know it's small, but it feels really big to me."*

*There was light applause around the circle and plenty of smiles to go around. A man across from Jamie spoke up.*

*"I don't believe in small progress. We should celebrate every accomplishment, no matter how we perceive it. Three days is a big deal!"*

*Jamie allowed herself to show a small smile to the group, but in reality, her chest swelled with pride.*

· · · · ● · ● · ● · ● · ·

Now armed with the knowledge that although numbing behaviors can seem right in the moment, they do little to help with recovery, let's move on to the behaviors that do help!

# 7

—·—

## SELF CARE

It is baffling how often we are advertised with self-care how-to's and the knowledge that self-care is relevant and yet, we struggle to fit it into our daily routines. We will sit down to make a plan of self-care and perform it for maybe a week, and then completely drop it in favor of working a few more hours at our job or running errands. The time has come to make self-care a part of your daily routine, just like brushing your teeth or showering. Without the necessary self-care, you will only create more stress for yourself, essentially slowing down your healing process from making much progress. How can we make more time in your day for self-care, and in what forms?

## Incorporating Self-Care Routines

Although it would be nice, self-care doesn't have to be big and extravagant like it is sometimes portrayed to be. In its purest sense, self-care is just taking care of yourself in a way that is healthy and in a way that you enjoy. For instance, if you're eating something healthy but you don't like it, try substituting it for something else that is healthy, but you actually enjoy eating. Perhaps try different seasonings, or a different way of preparing the food. If you have the time, energy, and money to do something huge for self-care such as going on a shopping trip or indulging on a spa day, then absolutely do that! But it's important to note that self-care isn't just about that. It's about the little things that you can do throughout the day to take care of yourself.

• • • ● ● • ● • • •

*Jamie started to feel a little frustrated with herself. It was the second time this week she had forgotten to do her mindfulness exercises, and it was only Wednesday.*

*She felt a panic start to set in, but before it could, she started to take some deep breaths. "Everyone makes mistakes. That doesn't mean you're failing to make progress," she whispered to herself.*

*Gently lowering herself into her seat, she closed her eyes. She may have missed her mindfulness exercises a few times, but that doesn't mean she had to quit. She was going to choose forgiveness.*

• • • ● ● • ● • • •

After reading this chapter, try shaking up your daily routine with your own ideas of self-care. If you really like bike rides, try biking to errands instead of driving. Try using the time you would be using to stream Netflix to take a bubble bath instead.

**Food as Fuel**

It may be tempting for speed and convenience to eat fast food frequently, but try substituting eating out for homecooked meals. It's important that the food you put in your body is nutritious and has variety to it. Making sure you have different fruits, vegetables, and proteins every day is a good way to ensure variety within your diet. As mentioned earlier, if you don't like a certain food, try experimenting with it. You don't always have to have it cooked the exact same way. If you find out that you don't like it, you can replace it with a different food that has a similar nutrition label to what you're looking for. For instance, if you don't like bananas, you can try eating cantaloupe, which is a food that is also rich in potassium. You should make your diet enjoyable while at the same time making sure you get all your vitamins and nutrients.

As it is important to have a healthy diet, it's also important to note that it's okay to eat unhealthy foods occasionally, as well. A candy bar every now and then as a treat is nothing to feel guilty over, as long as you don't make junk foods a staple in your main diet. With this, be wary of emotional eating. Eat when you are physically hungry, rather than when you are sad, bored, lonely, tired, or angry.

**Importance of Sleep**

Sleep is hard enough to come by nowadays, but some people with PTSD experience nightmares based on their traumatic experiences. These nightmares get so bad that these individuals can do everything they can to prevent going to sleep, including staying up for a day or two at a time to avoid them. Avoiding sleep in such a way is actually a destructive coping behavior, and can cause one's mental health to continue to decline. Sleep is important, especially during the recovery process. While you're asleep, your brain will solidify any progress you've made that day into long-term memory. If you don't sleep, then you don't get the opportunity to solidify that progress, and it's like taking a step back.

Nightmares are a bad experience, but there are ways in which you can increase the chance of preventing them. Performing meditation or mindfulness exercises right before bed can relax the body and mind and prepare you for rest. Avoiding food or substances, such as alcohol or caffeine, should also decrease your chances of having a nightmare. There's also the option of talking to your primary care provider. They will be able to talk out all of your options in great detail, and may be able to prescribe a medication that blocks out dreams entirely, if both of you deem it necessary.

**Exercise**

Finding time throughout your day to exercise is vital. This doesn't necessarily mean lifting weights or finding a personal trainer. Exercise, in its purest sense, just means getting your heart rate up for about 20 minutes a day.

For people recovering from trauma, it is recommended to perform yoga, walking, and deep stretches as your form of exercise. This acts in the same way that meditation and mindfulness exercises do, while also giving you the benefits of exercise. Luckily, all three of these types of exercises are things that are easily done and have varieties that can be done within the home. Your 20 minutes of walking can even be achieved just trying to get from place to place throughout the day!

While those exercises are recommended for individuals with PTSD, that doesn't mean that other exercises can't be used for self-care. If you have a home gym, you can certainly use that, or if you play any sports, such as soccer, football, or tennis, that works just as great! As long as you get your time in and you're enjoying yourself, it doesn't really matter what you're doing in the end.

## Stick to a Routine

Not knowing what your day is going to look like in advance can put unnecessary stress on yourself. While some spontaneity can be good, having your life be completely unstructured can lead to a chaotic lifestyle. With the parts of your life that are under your control, try changing this to be less stressful on your body and mind.

Start off small. Try waking up and going to bed around the same time every day. If you have trouble keeping track of the time when you're supposed to be going to bed, set an alarm 10 minutes before your designated time to go to sleep. This should allow you enough time to put on pajamas, take any medications, and do any other bedtime rituals you may have. After you've got your sleeping schedule down, try incorporating other consistencies in your schedule. If you bring work home, designate a specific time when you will be working. That way, you won't be working the entire time you're off the clock.

Routines don't have to be only time-based. It can also be along the lines of making sure you perform certain tasks everyday. For instance, shower, brush your teeth, and get dressed every single day, even if you have nothing going on that day. Even with the effort that it takes to perform these tasks, it will make you feel a little better after they've been completed.

## Meditate/Mindfulness

Meditation and mindfulness exercises have come up a lot so far, and that's because they are so important and incredibly helpful to those recovering from ACEs. If you haven't done either of these before, it doesn't take much to get into them.

When you're living with PTSD, it can often seem like you're still living in the past. Flashbacks, nightmares, and pain caused by ACEs make it appear that no progress is being made, like you're truly living in two different moments of time simultaneously. Becoming more mindful is a self-care practice that can help you alleviate that dreadful feeling of being unable to escape the past. Mindfulness grounds you in the present and brings attention to your physical body and the senses you are feeling in the current moment. This is important because PTSD can make you feel detached from your body, while mindfulness brings that attachment back.

As mentioned previously, there are many ways to go about bringing mindfulness into your daily life. There are YouTube videos of guided meditations one can watch and follow along. If you search for apps on your phone, you can find many dedicated to mindfulness practices. Mindfulness only takes a few minutes a day, and it can easily be done in between other tasks throughout your day!

## Music

It doesn't matter if you're listening to it, composing it, playing an instrument, or just singing along. Research has shown that music helps the healing process (Garrido et al., 2015). When it comes to the healing process, music is primarily used to process and express emotions associated with the traumatic events. It can also be used in group settings, where group connections can be made. This allows for people to feel less alone in their experiences.

In your daily life, try listening to music more. Make a playlist of some comforting songs that you can listen to on your way to work or while you're cooking dinner. You can make several different playlists for different moods, activities, or even days of the week! Try using apps like Pandora to find new music similar to the songs you know you already like.

If you're feeling adventurous, pick an instrument that you've always wanted to try learning. Teaching yourself a new instrument can be difficult, but rewarding if you remain consistent with your practice. If playing an instrument does not speak to you, there are many opportunities for adults to join choirs. Joining a choir means you can connect with others interested in the same things as you, possibly expanding your support system in the process.

**Spending Time with Others**

Speaking of support systems, spending time with others is another essential way of performing self-care. As human beings, we are social creatures. We thrive off of community and interaction. Being at home alone consistently is isolating. When you're with others, they can support you in your time of need and distract you when need-be.

In this day and age, it may feel like it's hard to find the time to spend with the people you care about. However, there are plenty of small things you can do to reach out to family and friends. If they live nearby, try having scheduled meals with them. Make every Thursday night a shared dinner where one of you cooks and the other brings dessert. If your loved one lives farther away, try scheduling an online hangout session. There are many platforms today that feature video chatting. Through video chatting, you don't have to only talk. You can participate in a knitting circle, watch a movie, paint, or several other activities that you could do together in person. If you're into playing video games as a hobby, many have online multiplayer options where you can play with your friends and chat with them at the same time.

If you truly do not feel like you have enough time in the day to make room for social interaction, sending a simple text to those you care about can go a long way.

## Consider Volunteer Work

A great form of self-care that is actually beneficial in more ways than one is volunteer work. Not only do you get to feel great for providing good services to those in need, but those individuals you helped will most definitely feel grateful in the end. It just leaves a general positive feeling to leave some good in the world.

For those who have never volunteered, it's easy to get started, and there's a wide variety of volunteer opportunities available out there. Searching the internet for volunteer opportunities near you is a good first step. You can also look to see what small businesses have to offer. Oftentimes, they will have flyers posted in their shops of local events being advertised that could use volunteers.

The possibilities for what one can do in volunteer work are truly endless. One can help with planning, gardening, serving food, playing music, building with material, taking care of animals, handing out advertisements, and much more. If you can think of a skill, there's pretty much an opportunity for you to volunteer for it. It's definitely worth looking at what your area has to offer in terms of volunteer work.

## Creative Outlet

Just like music, many other creative outlets serve the same purposes in terms of expressing emotions and creating community. What qualifies as something creative? Creative simply means something that has been created by an individual using their imagination. This means activities like writing, painting, pottery, acting, and cooking. Experiment and find things that you end up enjoying.

You can easily combine your creative outlet with spending time with others. Many groups exist in which the members do their creative activity together, even if it is an activity that can be done alone. For instance, knitting circles are made up of participants who knit while talking to each other. Members of these circles will trade advice on how to complete projects, where to get supplies, and support each other through their works. It's a great way to both pass the time in a relaxing way and experience the feeling of community. While knitting circles are one of the more popular examples of participating in a creative outlet with a group of people, you can do this with any other form of creativity. If you are interested in writing and know others who are also interested, you can start a writing group. For 15 minutes at a time, everyone can write on the same prompt, and then switch papers with someone else. Then, they can continue on with the story, or edit the paper. If no group seems to already exist in the area, feel free to create your own! Gather up some friends, decide on a meeting time, and create some rules agreed upon throughout the group.

**Spiritual Needs**

Spirituality is a sacred thing, and it comes in a variety of different forms. Some individuals don't feel as connected to spirituality as others are, which is absolutely normal. No matter your level of spirituality, you are completely valid. It's important to make sure your spiritual needs are met in order for self-care to happen.

Keep note that while spirituality and religion go hand in hand, they are not the same thing. Going to church every holy day may fulfill some individuals' spiritual needs, but not everyone's. For some, spirituality can mean feeling connected to the nature that surrounds their house. Dedicate some time to look into yourself and see what spirituality means to you. Mindfulness exercises will be helpful with this process. Once you have even a general idea of what spirituality means to you, the next step is deciding on how to meet your needs. Do you have to change something in your life to meet your spiritual needs? Is it a big or little change? Find support in your life as you do whatever it is that you must do to fulfill your spiritual needs.

**Reward Yourself**

Life may seem ruthless sometimes. There can be long stretches without any noticeable benefits ahead. That's why it's okay to take control and reward yourself when you go through times where you may feel like your progress is for nothing.

Set up habit trackers for other self-care essentials with personal goals on them. Make sure your goals are achievable. For instance, if you don't exercise at all right now, don't make one of your goals to complete a marathon by next week. A much more attainable goal would be to walk around the neighborhood every day for a week before increasing your level of exercise.

Rewards can be anything you want, so pick something you enjoy. It can be a food that you don't get often, an activity, or a break in between work sessions. If you want, you can set up your reward so that it matches the task in effort. If you keep up with self-care tasks for a week, you can treat yourself to a candy bar of your choosing. In contrast, if you keep up with self-care tasks for a year, you can treat yourself to a spa day, if you have the money and the desire to do so. Use a calendar if you choose to do this method to track reward levels over time.

Now that we are no longer putting self-care on the back burner, what else can be done to assist with the healing process?

# 8

— · —

## DOES RESILIENCE WORK?

*Jamie tossed her car keys on the coffee table and slumped onto her couch. Her neighbor wanted to start carpooling to the grocery store, but he never drove. It was bad enough that she had to drive every single time, but he never even offered to help pay for gas.*

*Still, she didn't want to speak up. Felt like she couldn't speak up. Roger has had some pretty rough times, so maybe he's just trying to get back on his feet. She would keep driving him for now.*

· · · ● · ● · ● · · ·

Resilience is your personal ability to face challenges thrown your way. In this case, these challenges are related to mental health specifically, such as coping with mental illness symptoms. It is one of our most powerful defenses. Resilience works wonders for progress. Increasing resilience is the key to thriving despite life circumstances. The more resilience someone has, the more life adversities they are able to handle with less negative effects on their health. Resilience is the strength within us that allows us to keep fighting. On top of ways to increase your resilience, there are ways to increase your overall mental health through added self-care routines. These self-care routines are different from the previous chapter's because they are more focused specifically on self-love. What do resilience and mental health self-care routines look like in daily life?

## Mental Health Self-Care Routines

Developing a mental health self-care routine with a focus on increasing resiliency is essential to claiming happiness, success, and sustainable, functional relationships with others. It focuses on self-love and health of the mind, rather than the overall health of the body in its entirety. While other types of self-care need to be done consistently for a long period of time, this type of self-care only needs to be done for a little while before you get the full effects. After you get the full effects, you may need to perform the self-care every once in a while to check in with yourself, but it does not need to be as consistent as other types of self-care.

### Put a Name to Stress

Take the time to recognize what your body feels like when it is under stress. Do you notice a lot of increased tension in your muscles compared to usual? Some people have acne breakouts when they are under long periods of stress. Others feel increasingly tired or may have a change in appetite. While there are some general common identifiers of stress, not everyone is going to have the same reaction to it. How does your body react?

Not only will your body start to work differently than it usually does, you may consciously do things differently. You may choose to do things that are a comfort to you in order to ease the stress you are beginning to feel. Ever notice that you seem to eat more chocolate around the times you have more stress in your life? Or do you always rewatch your favorite movie when things start to seem out of control? Look out for your pattern behaviors to see what you do when you get stressed. We tend to get into routines when we get stressed. Some of these behaviors are performed to keep us calm, while others are performed to push us into high gear.

## Strengthen Your Ability to Relax

Find a variety of ways that work at making you calm. Make sure that they cover a vast number of situations, since there are many different situations in which you could need to feel relaxed. If you're at home, you may have more opportunities to feel calm than when you're out in public, so make sure you have all of your bases covered.

For instance, when you're at home, you may be able to make yourself a cup of tea if a hot drink helps relax you. In public, you may not have the same opportunity to drink that warm cup of tea to settle your nerves. To combat this, rely on other ways to calm yourself, not just one or two ways. For those who like music and feel connected to it, try humming as a method of relaxing in public. Deep breathing exercises can also be performed while you're out and about.

Make a list of all the possible calming methods you can think of, and mark them as you try them. Which ones on your list worked and which ones didn't? In what situations are you able to use the ones that did work?

## Power up Your Positive Emotions

Previously, we focused on all of the negative emotions you may feel due to your traumatic experiences. Now, it is the time to focus on the opposite side of the spectrum. Research has shown that positive emotions have been able to benefit a variety of different aspects of health, not just mental health (Tugade et al., 2004). Take advantage of your positive emotions such as happiness, joy, laughter, and gratitude and the beneficial effects they have on your healing process.

To feel the effects of these emotions, you truly don't have to do anything. If you've done other things for your healing process, these emotions will come naturally to you, and hopefully, often. However, if you want to increase the amount of time you feel positive emotions, try listing the pros of feeling them. For instance, they make you feel good, they make you appreciate the little things more, you find that you garden more when you're happy, and other such strengths. Then, find the time to go out and do the things that trigger your positive emotions.

If you like baking but don't normally do it because you don't eat a lot of sweets, give away the food items you bake to your friends, family, and neighbors.

## Practice Self-Compassion and Loving Self-Talk

Self-compassion and loving self-talk fit well with what is taught in cognitive-behavioral therapy. You must work to reframe the negative things you think about yourself. Instead of saying things such as "I am unhappy with my body," try substituting that thought with "my body does what it can so that I am alive and healthy." These thoughts of self-compassion can be created out of any negative thought. While it is best to get the help of a cognitive-behavioral therapist, you are able to do this by yourself.

You can also show self-compassion in other ways. Allow yourself to make mistakes as you would allow others. Give yourself the same grace and respect that you give the people around you. You are worthy and deserving of it.

When you believe you are ready to try it, give yourself compliments. They don't have to be of a certain frequency or of a certain type, just whatever you feel is right for you. If one day you look in the mirror and think an outfit looks great on you, tell yourself that. If you did something kind for a stranger, it's good to acknowledge that you did something nice.

## Establish Boundaries

Boundaries are one of the most important aspects of self-care for mental health. You deserve to establish boundaries for yourself. If you let someone cross your boundaries, then you risk your mental health worsening.

Your boundaries are your own personal limits. They may be your triggers, things that you're uncomfortable with, or things that you have never tried and are unwilling to try. Boundaries are fluid. Something that you may have been fine with at one point, you may have a boundary around now, and vice versa.

Create either a physical or mental list of your boundaries. Listen to your body whenever someone tries to cross one. Stand up for yourself if someone tries to break through your boundaries. They are your boundaries for a reason, and you should demand respect for them. If you let one person cross your boundaries, you may have others try to cross them, or that one person may try to continuously try to cross your boundaries. Hold firm, and know your limits.

• • • ● • ● • • •

*Jamie pulled into the parking lot of her apartment complex. Roger opened the car door to leave.*

*"Wait, Roger, I wanted to tell you something before you left."*

*He looked back at Jamie, then got back into the car. "What's on your mind, hun?"*

*She grimaced at the nickname. "I'm not going to be able to carpool to the grocery store anymore. Also, I would really prefer it if you didn't call me 'hun'."*

*Roger popped open the car door again. "Well, I appreciate all the rides you've given me, miss."*

*Jamie sighed. They would have to work on nicknames.*

• • • ● • ● • • •

## Set Goals

At some point during the healing process, take the time to re-evaluate your values. You will have changed a lot as a person, and there's a good chance that some of your values will have originally come from your family. These values either may have been forced on you, or you could have taken them on because you had no experience with other options.

Either way, you may have strayed from those beliefs since then, and it is time to look at what you stand for now. Note that it's okay if nothing about your values has changed after evaluation or everything has changed. The values you hold as a person do not define you, what you do with them does.

After you have completed the evaluation of your values, set a few goals around your new values. When setting goals, make sure they are specific, measurable, attainable, relevant, and time-based (SMART). SMART goals assure that you can actually reach your goals. If your value is family, an example of a SMART goal you could make is "every day this week, I am going to spend at least 30 minutes playing a board game with my family." Setting these goals will allow you to reconnect with your values, and give you little things to work toward every day.

**Visualization**

Don't lose sight of your goals. It can be easy to make goals and only get halfway through before you get bored of them and don't follow through. However, research has shown that those who perform visualization exercises are more likely to stick with their goals and complete them (Adams, 2009). Remain on target. When you make your goals, make them based on things you believe you will want long-term. Visualizing your goals gives you a full picture of what the end product looks like and the steps to get there, giving you expectations on the way. Using every sense in your visualization process allows for a fully formed picture.

During your meditation and mindfulness exercises, envision what your end goal will look like. What impact does your goal have on your environment after it is is completed? What impacts are you hoping it will have? How do you expect to feel after you have reached your goal? If you are having trouble doing this on your own, there are several apps that can help you.

Once you have fully explored the scenario of your finished goal and its aftereffects, send the positive energy you hope it will have into the universe. Similarly to a version of the release stage of processing emotions, you can send out this positive energy by imagining it leaving your body and entering the universe. Having a general expectation of your goals gives you a better idea of what to aim for, making it easier to achieve.

## Affirmations

Combine this visualization of your goals with daily affirmations. Going in with a positive mindset decreases the possibility of discouragement and abandonment of your projects. It also increases the amount of effort you are going to put into achieving your goals, making it more likely that you will hit them. Having daily affirmations makes the task at hand appear less scary, so in result, we feel like we have an easier time achieving them (Moore, 2021).

Write down your affirmations on sticky notes, on your calendar, or your daily planner. These affirmations can be things such as "I know how to accomplish my goal," and "I am strong enough to reach my goal." Consistency is important for you to reach your goal. Make affirmations that are specific to you. What aspects of goal completion are important to you? Focus on those aspects in your affirmations.

Sometimes, you may find that affirmations are hard for you to accomplish due to negative internal responses you have embedded inside. If you believe this may be the case for you, don't be afraid to reach out to a therapist for guidance as you create affirmations.

## Journaling and Emotion Processing

A good way to destress from a long day, or any type of day, is to process your emotions through journaling. Go through your day and write about anything of importance. Focus on the things you believe went well, and make a section dedicated to gratitude. Gratitude has shown to have a positive impact on the symptoms of PTSD (Smith, 2014). What were you grateful for throughout the day? Being reminded of what we are grateful for leads us to focus on the aspects of our lives that we believe are working right for us.

Use this time to also process any negative emotions you may have had throughout your day. Daily life is not free of annoyance and frustration. Once you feel like you have appropriately processed through any negative emotions, you have the option of performing the release step of processing emotions. Tear out the pages of the journal you had written on, if you want, and throw them away. Burn the pages at a bonfire and roast sausages over the flames. Meditate while imagining all the negative energy from those feelings exiting your body.

**Make Time for Solitude: Meditation**

We've talked a lot about meditation and mindfulness exercises, but did you know that there are different types of meditations that help with different aspects of the mind? The next time you settle in to do your meditation, try searching for a guided meditation meant to improve an area that you're struggling with. Maybe you're having trouble falling asleep at night, or your creative juices don't seem to be flowing like they used to be. You'd be amazed at the amount of guided meditations out there, and the vast amount of topics they cover.

Use your meditation practice to boost whatever it is you're working on when you're not focusing on being mindful. If you're working on a creative project in your free time and want an extra boost, creative guided meditations might be just what you're looking for. However, you are definitely more than welcome to focus on separate things through your meditation and other projects, as well. It might take longer to do, but it can be worth it in the end when you improve multiple things at the same time!

**Create a Community**

Another hugely important thing to remember during the recovery process is that you're not alone and you are never alone. Welcome support in your life by joining some sort of community. This community does not necessarily have to be related to your mental health, although it is encouraged. Being a part of a community in general is just so that you can get the feeling that you are a part of something bigger. Joining some form of community will allow you to build connections with others.

If you do join a community that is specifically about mental health, such as Alcoholics Anonymous (AA) meetings, group therapy, or a support group, then you get the added bonus of having others who have gone through similar situations as you. You will be able to relate to the experiences that the participants of these communities have had, strengthening your bonds and adding to your support systems.

Sometimes, a community does not necessarily exist in your area for a topic that you are looking for. Don't lose hope! If you want to put in the time and effort, you can create your own community to connect with others who live in your area.

## Resilience Training

The resilience inside of us is not a personality trait or characteristic we have. We do not have a set amount of resilience at birth. There are certain factors we have growing up that can increase our resistance. These factors are related to our home environments and social relationships. As we grow into our adult years, there are resilience exercises we can do to build up the skill. They can be learned in therapy settings, or searched for online. We will review a few of these exercises shortly, but first, let's dive deeper into the meaning of resilience.

### What It Means to Be Resilient

In some contexts, being resilient means being tough, fearless, and courageous. There are a few holes in this definition in relation to psychology. For one, the word "tough" insinuates a need to be strong and hard-willed, when in fact, the opposite is quite true. It's okay to recognize the need to be soft. You have been through hardships, and sometimes, remaining strong all of the time is hard within itself. Secondly, while being fearless and courageous on your healing journey would be ideal, it can be a scary process. To reiterate, you've been through a lot. Being afraid is a part of the journey, and that's okay, too.

A much better way to describe resilience is "persistence." You bounce back, even after you have challenge after challenge thrown your way. You take the opportunity to learn from the moment, and use what you've learned for any similar situations that may occur in the future. Being resilient is not giving up when you want to. How can you increase your resilience to gain its benefits?

**Resilience Exercises to Practice**

There are many exercises you can do to increase your resilience. These exercises are often taught in therapy settings to better prepare individuals for the next time they may face adversities. However, there are some you can do without the help of a mental health professional.

When it comes to how the world works, we tend to view it one of two ways: either you have complete control of your actions and the things that happen to you, or luck and chance are a major influence on the events in your life. For example, if you get a good grade on a test, you can either say it's because you are smart and you studied really hard, or you can say you got lucky that the test was easy and you just happened to know the answers. Viewing this situation as the former is an example of an internal locus of control, whereas viewing it as the latter is an example of an external locus of control. In terms of increasing resilience, it is better to have an internal locus of control. With this type of viewpoint, you feel like your actions are more meaningful. If you have an external locus of control, you are more likely to feel like none of your actions matter at all, so there is no point in putting any effort into them. Try to develop an internal locus of control rather than an external locus. Give your actions meaning to increase resilience.

Another exercise you can do is reframing your thoughts of "I should do" into "I could do." When you go into an activity with the mindset that you should be doing the activity, it makes it appear to be more of a duty or a chore. With that in mind, you may develop a negative attitude toward the activity. This is especially important if the activity that needs to be performed truly is a duty or something that isn't necessarily considered fun. When you reframe the thought into "I could do," then it becomes more of a choice, even if it actually isn't. We view choices much more positively than we view things we have to do. While doing things for your healing process, thinking of them as something you could do makes them feel like less of a hassle, and gives you more strength to be able to do them.

Now that your trauma recovery tool kit is filled with therapy options, self-care routines, and mental health routines, how do you know that you are healing?

# 9

## RECOVERING FROM CHILDHOOD TRAUMA

*Jamie steps on the scale. Her clothes have felt a lot looser lately. It couldn't be, though. It has to be her imagination. She hasn't successfully lost weight since she started gaining it all those years ago. But still, she felt like she had a little extra room in the clothes she owned for years.*

*She gasped. 14 pounds lighter? How could that be? Jamie rushed over to her mirror. She no longer looked like her ordinary self. The Jamie looking back at her was not the Jamie who drank beer and overate everytime she wanted to forget her parents. This Jamie was not the same Jamie who did everything for her boyfriend who wouldn't do anything for her in return. No, the woman looking back at her was demanding respect, and she was getting it. This Jamie was eating vegetables and practicing yoga and she was proud of herself.*

*A hand reached toward the reflection in the mirror. She may not have been completely in love with herself right then, but she sure was proud of where she was.*

. . . . ● . ● . . .

## The Signs of Success

You've come a long way already. Where does the road end? Healing isn't exactly a process that has a straightforward end. There is no definitive end to healing from parental trauma. It's a process that you have to keep working for continuously.

Even though it sounds hopeless, working toward healing is not. The healing process gets easier over time. When you have to work toward healing continuously, it's more like routine maintenance work. There might be a chance that you relapse at one point, and that's okay. You might return to a destructive coping behavior for a brief period of time, or have a PTSD flashback after not having one for months. Just because something seemingly goes wrong after everything has been going much better for a long time doesn't mean you have failed in any way. It just means you are a normal human being, and that your trauma has really impacted you. You must remain persistent with your self-care routines, and be extra kind to yourself if you do have a moment where you seem to falter.

In this continuous personal journey, there are many signs that you are going in the right direction. Coming across these on your own should signify to you that you've made great progress on your healing journey. However, once you've become aware of them, you can make an effort to try to reach them, as well. They have a dual purpose, in this sense.

## Acceptance

Acceptance is in reference to the traumatic events which have occurred to you in the past. In the beginning of the healing process, some individuals may be in denial that the events have happened at all. They may make excuses for their abuser or abusers, and come up for reasons for why their behavior may have happened. In other denial situations, the individual may recognize that something bad has happened, but does not label it as "abuse" or "traumatic." To them, it is just an unfortunate thing that happened to them while they were a kid, but they do not believe it impacts them in any such way today. Individuals who start the healing process in denial are often referred by their loved ones to start the healing, because they themselves don't believe something needs to be healed in the first place.

Acceptance is the ability to acknowledge these events for what they were. They were traumatic, they were painful, you shouldn't have gone through them, and you are still feeling the impacts of them today.

This is not an easy truth, and therefore not an easy thing for people to accept. Some people are only willing to accept parts of it at a time, and that's okay. Everyone comes to terms with it at their own pace.

## Welcoming Support

As the opposite of the destructive coping behavior, isolation, it is great to welcome support into your life. Too often people isolate themselves when they begin to feel the effects of their childhood traumas. When you bring others into your life to help you carry your burdens, it shows your personal growth. It shows that you are acknowledging the fact that you cannot perform the healing process on your own.

There is a key word here: welcome. This insinuates that you want the support, that when you see it, you greet it with open arms. You cannot acknowledge that you have to get support, but feel cold to the idea of it. There is a huge difference between getting support because you want to and getting support because you feel like you have to. Both will evidently help in the healing process, but wanting to get help will not only show that you have improved, but it will increase the effectiveness of getting support. You will be willing to get more support, and for a wider variety of things than if you were to get support only because you knew you needed it or if because someone forced you.

Welcome support from a variety of sources. Get it from family, friends, peers from your support groups, and any mental health professionals you may come into contact with. The more people you find yourself welcoming support from, the more comfortable you become with the idea of sharing your burdens.

## Reasonable Expectations

As a species, we tend to set higher standards for ourselves than we do for others. "We're all rough drafts of the people we're still becoming" (Goff, 2018). We judge our work more critically, and will even go to the lengths of discrediting the praises of others if we believe we do not deserve them. Our expectations of ourselves can become even harsher when we've grown up with parents who had unreasonably high expectations of us. Those unreasonably high expectations transfer to us, and we become even more critical of ourselves than what we may have already been.

Being able to have reasonable expectations of ourselves looks like recognizing our abilities and being able to accept praise when it is due. Sometimes, this praise comes from yourself, and is not just exclusively from those around us.

Having reasonable expectations for yourself comes from acknowledging that you are constantly changing. Yes, this project you have been working on may need improvement, but it is the best work you could have provided at the moment and you should be proud of yourself for that. You are not a perfect human being. In fact, no one is. Give yourself the same grace you would give anyone else.

Make sure that you have reasonable expectations for yourself in all aspects of life, not just when it comes to any projects you may be working on. For instance, it's an unreasonable expectation to believe that you will begin to heal immediately upon starting the healing process. It takes time, and everyone's process is unique. Give yourself these personal graces, as well.

**Forgiveness**

Holding in resentments for the things that have happened to you in the past is essentially the same thing as processing a negative emotion, but never moving past it. "Resentment is like taking a poison and expecting it to have an effect on others" (The Chopra Well, 2020). Learn to forgive the events in your past. The things that happened to you were horrible and should have never occurred, but the events of the past cannot change. If you keep those resentments locked away, it will block your progress.

There is a difference between forgiving the events and forgetting the events. Even if you forgive the events, you do not have to forget them. In fact, forcing yourself to forget them can also be harmful. These events are real, and they happened to you. They are something you must continually work toward getting better, and you can't work toward getting better if you are attempting to forget the events.

Forgiveness can be hard to achieve, but it is something you must come to terms with eventually. Take your time with learning how to forgive the situation. Remember that forgiveness does not equate to weakness. In this case, it means a chance at peace.

## Sharing Experience with Others

Similar to welcoming support, feel comfortable with sharing what you have gone through with others. People with experiences like yours can learn and grow from your stories. By sharing, you might help out someone in a support group or group therapy that you participate in. You might be the connection that makes someone feel less alone in the world, and also feel more connected to others in the process.

There are different levels of sharing your experiences. If you're only comfortable sharing it with the people within your support systems, then do so. There is nothing wrong with remaining at this comfort level. However, others may feel okay with sharing with a wider range of people. Some individuals may feel the need to share their experiences with a large audience, such as through public speaking. This way, they can reach through to a bigger crowd, possibly making more people feel less alone in the process. Doing this is a form of social activism, and isn't for everyone. Some people may even go as far as to share their stories through publishing books or going on talk shows to reach an even wider audience.

While there are many options in sharing your experiences with others, simply telling your story to those around you is all you need to do in order to show that you've made good progress. The other options may reach wider audiences, but can be quite anxiety-inducing, and are therefore not for everyone. No one is obligated to do anything based on the experiences they have had.

## Developing a Strong Relationship with Yourself

Out of all the relationships that may become damaged because of the trauma you have been put through, the one that might need the most repair is the relationship you have with yourself.

There is a good chance that due to your traumas, you have an altered perception of yourself today. Your view of yourself has been heavily influenced by the events of the past. Now that you have the time and the awareness of the effects of these events, take the time to really get to know yourself.

Start off small. Get to know your likes and dislikes. Sometimes, you are shaped in a way to have the same likes and hobbies as your parents, even if you don't truly desire those things. Sort out which of your likes are actually your likes and which ones are the ones you were just told to like because someone influential in your life liked them. Once you've done that, continue on with things such as your personal style, your aspirations, and your goals.

During this time of self-exploration, make sure to try out new things. Something you may have never considered before may become a quick favorite. You might discover that sushi is actually the best food you have ever eaten, or that rock climbing is truly the worst activity you have done. Now is the time to explore and give definition to "you."

## Letting Go of Insecurities

An unfortunate effect of ACEs is low self-esteem. This comes with many insecurities about oneself. Insecurities tend to collect over the years and eventually stack upon each other. They can truly make somebody dislike the body and mind they are living in.

You can tell progress is being made when these insecurities you have had for years on end finally dissipate. Maybe you notice that it no longer bothers you how you don't have a thigh gap, or you realize that you actually really like the way that you laugh. This change isn't going to occur overnight, as much as you may want it to. It's going to take a lot of persistent hard work to start to fall in love with yourself.

Start by reframing the way you look at your insecurities. You don't have to go straight from a negative mindset to a positive one. Changing to a neutral mindset is the true step you want to take, and it is the actual end goal of changing your insecurities. While using your insecurities to your advantage in the process of loving yourself would be ideal, you only need to reframe your insecurities to something different. For instance, if you're insecure about your grades and believe that they could be better, reframe this insecurity as you are trying your best in school, and your effort is what truly counts in the long run. If you continue to work at reframing your insecurities in such a way, it will soon come naturally to you.

## Setting up Boundaries

Establishing boundaries is something that was covered under mental health self-care, and must be worked on in general in order to add to the healing process. However, if you start noticing you setting up boundaries automatically with the people in your life, that is a good sign. Boundaries becoming a part of your routine shows a healthy relationship between you and your limits.

Setting up your boundaries looks like many different things, and you aren't always aware that you're doing it. If you're in a group setting where they are having a conversation about something that may trigger a PTSD flashback in you, you have a few options for setting up a boundary in this situation. Some people may excuse themself from the scenario, recognizing that they do not owe it to the group to be a part of the conversation if they are not comfortable with the subject matter. Others may ask the group not to talk about that subject around them, acknowledging that they are not a burden and deserve to feel safe in group environments.

If something doesn't feel right, don't be afraid to say no. You can do this figuratively, with your actions, or say this literally, by denying out loud. In your world, you get to set the rules, but you also need to make sure they are enforced, as well.

## Stop Judging, Apologizing, or Seeking Approval

Too often do people living with the repercussions of ACEs view themselves too harshly. They see themselves as weak and do whatever they can to please the people in their lives. Submission to someone else is the only goal, and it's the only way to make the pain stop.

It's a really good sign when you begin to notice a decrease in these things. Your harsh self-critiques have gone down in favor of an increase in loving self-talk. You no longer constantly seek approval from others and therefore, do not aim to do the impossible to please your peers. You don't apologize for the things that are either out of your control, or that you don't need to apologize for because they are not mistakes.

Once you've lived through at least one ACE, you can tend to feel guilty for the things you do. Things that are typically seen as mistakes, accidents, or even just normal behavior can be made to believe that they are wrong and should not be performed. For instance, accidentally breaking a dish, or even a child raising their voice because they got excited could get punished. It's like these actions are completely unacceptable. It takes a lot of time to unlearn these myths. It's okay to make mistakes and perform other such behaviors. Improvement is shown once you begin to stop critiquing yourself and apologizing for these behaviors, and when you stop seeking for the approval of your peers and authority figures.

## Loving Intentionally and Unconditionally

Loving freely might be a difficult thing to build up to when you've had walls surrounding you for so long. That's why it's a good sign of progress. What does loving intentionally and unconditionally mean, though, and who are you supposed to be loving in such a way? First and foremost, you should be choosing who gets your love. You choose the people you surround yourself with, and you make sure you give those people love. Secondly, loving intentionally and unconditionally means that you love without holding back aspects of yourself or holding expectations of the other person.

While there are no expectations on who you should love or how you should express that love, there is a general rule of thumb with which you should start: learn to love yourself the way you want to love others. Loving yourself with purpose is the true test of progress. Once you can do that, you are well on your way to becoming happy and healthy.

# 10

## COMPLICATED PARENT RELATIONSHIPS

*Jamie sat in the cafe, her leg bouncing wildly. Would she recognize him? Would he recognize her? She had moved out of her mother's house when she was 18, but she'd been even younger when she last saw her father.*

*At age 15, her father moved to a different country on a business opportunity. Since all of her connections remained in the United States, Jamie was to live with her mother full time. Her father did not fight this, and that was the last time she saw or heard from him. Until this exact moment.*

*Her first thought was that he looked old. Time did not treat her old man well. He had the assistance of a cane now, something Jamie would have to get used to. The thought of it almost brought a smile to her face. This man hobbling toward her used to bring fear, and now he could barely walk! The scene was almost comical, in a sadistic way.*

*Any urge to laugh at the situation completely dissipated once her father sat across from her. That old fear struck her. No, it wasn't fear. It was dread. Dread for this moment she had willingly created settled into her stomach. She suddenly didn't feel very hungry.*

*"Hello Jamie," her father said.*

*"Hi dad."*

• • • • • • • • • •

Once therapy, self-care, and mental health routines are firmly set and progress has been made, people may choose to work on their relationship with their toxic parent. It's important to note that this choice is completely up to the individual. The healing process does not come to an end once you build a new relationship with your toxic parent. You may decide that you want to try having your parent heavily involved in your life, only partly involved in your life, or maybe not involved at all, and all of those decisions are valid. You and only you get to decide what type of relationship you want from your parental unit.

Each decision has its own pros and cons. For some, reconciliation brings closure and can create a parental relationship that was lacking during childhood. For others, attempting a parental relationship will only dig up bad memories. This does not mean that they have failed during the healing process. You do not owe your toxic parent a relationship. Only proceed if you feel like it is the best option for you.

## Establish Strong Boundaries

When going to meet with your toxic parent, you are going to need to establish strong boundaries. Your mental health is what matters most in this situation, and you need to protect it. These boundaries are going to be different from the boundaries you set up on a day-to-day basis, although there may be some crossover.

Why are new boundaries needed? Overall, the situation is going to be much different than anything you've experienced. Facing someone who may play a role in some of your traumas can take a lot of courage, and can be anxiety inducing. Due to this, you want to prepare yourself in any way you can. The protection of your mental health is the top priority in this scenario.

Once you have your boundaries set, remain true to them. The transition from childhood into adulthood is hard for parents to process. Even when their children are well into adulthood, they may continue to see them as children. This may cause parents to frequently overstep the child's boundaries, as they are used to a time when they did not have that sort of thing in between them. Be assertive with your boundaries. If your toxic parent happens to still view you as they did when you were a child, they may revert back to old behaviors. Remember that you are an adult now who is capable of making your own decisions. Do not let them attempt to make decisions for you, as this will let them regain the power in your life that they once had over you.

In the scenario of meeting your toxic parent, you want to remain in control. This is for the sake of your own wellness and safety. There is expected to be some overlap between your everyday boundaries and the boundaries you put up between you and your parent. What are the similarities and differences between these boundaries? What specific scenarios are they used for when it comes to meeting your toxic parent for the first time in a long time? Let's look at each of these further in depth.

## Set Ground Rules

Before you even meet up with your parent, it is a necessity to set ground rules. These ground rules need to be both for yourself and for the interactions between you and your parent.

Setting ground rules for yourself prepares you for what is to come. As this is most likely an experience you have not had yet, you won't be completely sure of how you will react once seeing your parent. Create ground rules such as "I will call my best friend if I feel like I am in trouble" in order to make you feel safe. Make sure to set other ground rules with yourself, preparing for how you will react in certain situations. If you feel scared, will you promise yourself to leave the situation or call someone who makes you feel safe? If you feel angry, will you do quick breathing exercises or excuse yourself to calm down?

It's equally important, if not more, to set ground rules with your parent. This requires an open dialogue before seeing them in person. These ground rules will be more based on the interaction between the two of you. If your parent breaks a ground rule, you have the power to walk away from the situation because they broke your trust. An example of this type of ground rule would be "I do not want to talk about this particular event, as it is triggering to me. If you do not respect the fact that I don't want to talk about it, I will leave the lunch early." Make as many ground rules as you need, make them clear to the parent, and once again, make them before you meet up. This will give the parent time to make their own ground rules for themself if need be. Remember that you are the one in control of the situation. Don't be afraid to say no, and don't seek their approval.

**Avoid Parenting the Parent**

Think of all of the responsibilities that come with raising a child. There are the physical necessities, such as making sure the child has food, water, and shelter, and there are the emotional necessities, such as teaching the child how to live in society and providing them with love. As the child in the parent-child relationship, it is not your responsibility to raise the parent. However, some have been put into the position of having to raise the parent, when that is not the role of the child. Raising the parent in any capacity forces the child to mature a lot faster than they would naturally. They don't get to experience childhood like they would if the roles were reversed.

If you raised your parent when they should have been raising you, avoid raising them when you see them again. Take this opportunity to live as the child in your relationship. Now, this doesn't mean you should revert back to the youth you didn't get to live out fully, but more like don't let your parent only see you when they need to borrow money from you. Your parent shouldn't need reminders on how to behave in public from you, or need you to fix all of their problems for them.

Moving on from trying to fulfill the role of parent to settling into your true role as child can be difficult. Both you and your parent have become used to the roles you have settled into previously, and having to relearn a new role like that is going to take some time to get used to. If you are regularly going to therapy, consider asking your therapist for help during this difficult transition. Get their advice and support during this time, as it will certainly not be easy trying to avoid old patterns of behavior.

**Learn to Recognize Cyclic Patterns of Abuse**

One of the reasons why the blame game doesn't work is because even if your parent is the one who directly abused you, there may be an outside influence on your parent that caused their behavior. For instance, your parent may have been living with a mental illness, or perhaps they were abusing drugs. These stressors, among others, can increase the chances of that individual performing toxic behaviors. Just to clarify, though, if your parent has had an outside influence that may have increased their chances of abusive behaviors, it is not an excuse for the performance of those behaviors.

Since outside influences for abusive behaviors tend to stick around for long periods of time, they can lead to cyclic patterns of abuse. Cyclic patterns of abuse are patterns of abuse that one may find to happen over and over again, even if there have been attempts to end the cycle.

Learning how to recognize cyclic patterns before meeting with your parent would be advantageous to you. This way, you can see if your parent was possibly taking part in a cyclic pattern. If you believe that they were, you might consider looking into if they have broken the cycle or not. Breaking the cycle of behavior would be hard, but it is possible, with the right resources. Every situation is different, and requires a unique way of breaking the cycle. For a parent who was abusing substances, making sure they went to a rehabilitation center and that they've been working toward sobriety may be necessary before you agree to seeing them again.

If you believe that your parent was participating in cyclic patterns of abuse, and that they haven't done anything effective to break their patterns, it may be best to avoid seeing them for the time being. Since there is no change in the influence, there is no reason why your parent could not attempt to start up the abuse cycle again now that you're in their life again. Once again, your own wellness and personal safety come before anything else when it comes to seeing your parent again.

## Recognize Your Unfulfilled Needs

Look back at your parent-child relationship in the past and take note of the different things you feel like you didn't get from it. If you were not satisfied with your relationship as a child, what were the specific aspects typically seen in a parent-child relationship that were missing? Maybe you desired a more loving environment, or one that was less critical of your work. These are your unfulfilled needs.

Your unfulfilled needs leave you wanting more as you go into adulthood. There is this part of you that wants closure, and when you get the chance to see your parent again, you might get the opportunity to get that desired closure. Don't feel guilty if you go into this meeting with your parent wanting their love and approval. This is a normal thing to be feeling.

Do decide beforehand which of your unfulfilled needs you want your parent to be involved in. Are you going to only allow them a few of your needs to fulfill, or will you try to give them all that were left empty? After you've decided which needs you are comfortable with having your parent fulfill, it's time to decide how you want your parent to fulfill the needs. This is, in other words, deciding the role you want your parent to have in your life today. It is suggested to ease them back into your life, and therefore, into your needs. It has likely been a while since you've seen each other, and fulfilling another's needs is a lot of responsibility to give to one person. In the meantime, find another relationship that is able to fulfill your needs.

## Avoid Trying to "Fix" Your Parents

Now that you are in a healthier frame of mind and have a newly equipped set of coping skills, you may be tempted to share these methods with your parents in an attempt to help them heal as well. Why shouldn't you share the knowledge that helped you, especially with someone you wish to reconnect with?

Although it may be something you want to do and you are willing to do, do not try to move along their healing process or "fix" them in any capacity. Change cannot happen without the full participation and consent of the individual who is performing the change.

Think about how your own healing process started and where the journey has taken you thus far. Now, think about the parts of your journey that have had other people involved in it. What was their involvement? More likely than not, they were aides during your healing process, but you were still in charge. At any point in time, you could have changed your course of healing in any way, or stopped entirely. In comparison, think about all of the times, before or during your healing process, in which someone may have tried to force change upon you. You were probably hesitant to it, resistant to it even. The same would apply to trying to help your parent upon meeting them.

Also consider the fact that changing your parent is not your responsibility. If you were a child who was succumbed to having to raise the parent, "fixing" the parent falls under those types of responsibilities. The parent is the one who is supposed to guide the child through life and help them when they make mistakes, not vice versa. This is too much to ask of a child, even when they become an adult. At this point in time, the most you can do is bring up the suggestion that your parent may need help if you see them struggling, like someone may have done for you, but no more should be done if they refuse.

## Stick to Your Self-Care Routines

• • • • ● • ● • • • •

*"You know, I've grown a lot since those days. Or at least, I hope I have. Sometimes it keeps me up at night. How could I have ever been too busy for my own daughter?"*

*"Dad, just like I don't have to prove anything to you, you don't have to prove anything to me. Those times hurt. Whenever I was at your house, I was left starving. It was like I was completely nonexistent. I'm not going to pretend*

*that that didn't do anything to me. But I'm here because something inside of me still wanted to try to be a family, and I think something inside of you wanted to try, too." Jamie reached out her hand toward her dad. "I'm still scared that you're going to hurt me. I still feel cautious around you. I'm hoping that over time, we can write over the bad memories with much better ones. What do you say, dad?"*

*He didn't have to give her his answer in word. He grabbed her hand and gripped it tightly. His eyes became misty. With a nod of his head, she knew his answer.*

*Jamie was making amends with her past.*

· · · ● · ● · ● · ● · ● · · ·

Above all, it is vital to stick to your self-care routines throughout the process of meeting with your parent. This is going to be a stressful time for you, whether or not the meeting itself goes well, and so it becomes important now more than ever that you take care of yourself both mentally and physically.

See if during this time, there is room during your normal self-care routines for you to go the extra mile. For instance, you may need more support from your friends than usual, so don't be afraid to reach out more times throughout the week than you normally do. Now would be a great time to splurge on one of your big self-care trips, such as going to the spa, or perhaps going to the movie theater to see a film that just came out. This extra boost in your self-care can go a long way during this stressful time.

If you are afraid of the possibility of getting behind in your self-care routines, find a way to remain accountable for them. Your self-care is not something that should be sacrificed during this time. Have a trusted friend to check in on you every so often to make sure you've done certain tasks. You can also set alerts on your phone in order to get reminded to do your self-care without having to get outside help involved.

Remember that self-care includes any therapy you've been going to up to now in your healing process. Consult with your therapist to see what kinds of specific coping methods you can do at home to help you through this situation. It's a good idea to lean on them a little more than usual during this time. Along with staying on top of the skills you learn in therapy, give yourself plenty of time to process emotions. It may take more time than usual, as your emotions will most likely be conflicting with each other. You can be excited about the possibility of a reconnection with your parent, but anxious that your new relationship will look much like your old one.

# Conclusion

Trauma can be so deeply embedded in our mind and body that we have many ill effects from the experience. I am humbled by the list of unhealthy outcomes that can occur from childhood trauma. But this is not where the story ends. You also have the ability to recover and reclaim your life, and you have the skills set up to do so.

## How to Move Forward After this Book

Continue on with the steps the book has taught you. Don't lose sight of your self-care practices, even when things start to get tough. Self-care must be prioritized and is essential to the healing process. Make sure that you are also sticking to your mental health routines, as well, as they are equally important in your road to recovery. Try not to fall back into old habits, as they can make you take some steps back.

Check in with yourself and others. You might find out that a friend has gone through something similar to you, and they need a little push to get their healing process started. Be that push for them.

## Take Action Now

I challenge you to pick some items from each section to work on so you can increase your resilience and regain power over your life and health. Set some realistic, yet challenging, goals and write them down as affirmations. Refer to your aspirations daily and visualize in great detail the action you want to obtain. Keeping a habit tracker, gratitude journal, or getting an accountability buddy is a great way to stay on target. It may seem hard to get started, but the longer you wait, the worse your effects from the adverse childhood events you experienced will become. This is your sign to start your healing journey now.

· ◦ · ● ◦ ● ◦ ● · ◦ ·

It means so much to me that you have read this book. I know your time is precious, but I am hoping you can spare a few minutes to leave a review. I take all your feedback to heart and will read each and every review personally.

If you want to join my newsletter group to receive updates on new books and/or just feel like giving me any other feedback, please do not hesitate to reach out at Hello@healingfromfamilytrauma.com. Thank you, Christine A Fisher

# ABOUT THE AUTHOR

 I have been a nurse for 30+ years, most of them specializing in the Neonatal Intensive Care Unit (NICU). During my years of nursing, I have seen firsthand the lasting effects of trauma. A NICU admission is one of the most stressful life experiences one can encounter, and can be equated to a form of post-traumatic stress disorder (PTSD) in parents. Nurses guide patient care in such a way as to reduce trauma whenever possible, although some traumatic interactions are inevitable to provide life-saving care and treatments.

Learning about trauma-informed care in the NICU, was eye-opening for me. I had no idea that traumatic events at this early age could lead to higher rates of different diseases, obesity, and drug addiction as adults. Since unfortunately, trauma can be unavoidable at times, I compiled research to determine what can be done to improve resiliency and mitigate the aftereffects once trauma has occurred.

It is my wish that traumatic events didn't happen in the first place. However, it is my quest to provide support and assistance to those struggling with the aftereffects of trauma to include the caregivers and support people in their lives.

# References

Adams, A. J. (2009 December 3). *Seeing is believing: The power of visualization*. Psychology Today. https://www.psychologytoday.com/us/blog/flourish/200912/-seeing-is-believing-the-power-visualization

*Adverse childhood experiences (ACEs) and their impact on brain development*. (2018 May 11). Maryland Coalition of Families. http://www.mdcoalition.org/blog/adverse-childhood-experiences-aces-and-their-impact-on-brain-development

*Anxiety and panic attacks*. (2021 February) Mind. https://www.mind.org.uk/information-support/types-of-mental-health-problems/anxiety-and-panic-attacks/panic-attacks/

Baxter, M. G., & Croxson, P. L. (2012). Facing the role of the amygdala in emotional information processing. *Proceedings of the National Academy of Sciences of the United States of America*, 109(52), 21180-21181. https://-doi.org/10.1073/pnas.1219167110

*CDC-Kaiser ACE study*. (2021 April 6). Centers for Disease Control and Prevention. https://www.cdc.gov/violenceprevention/aces/about.html?CDC_AA_refVal=https%3A%2F%2Fwww.cdc.gov%2Fviolenceprevention%2Faces-study%2Fabout.html

*Children and trauma*. (2011). American Psychological Association. https://www.apa.org/pi/families/resources/children-trauma-update

Chopra Well, The. (2020 May 27). *10 Min meditation - gratitude - daily guided meditation by Deepak Chopra.* [Video]. YouTube. https://www.youtube.com/watch?v=WIX05kY7oBk

*Cognitive processing therapy (CPT).* (2017 May). American Psychological Association. https://www.apa.org/ptsd-guideline/treatments/cognitive-processing-therapy

*Eye movement desensitization and reprocessing (EMDR) therapy.* (2017 May). American Psychological Association. https://www.apa.org/ptsd-guideline/treatments/eye-movement-reprocessing

*Fast facts.* (2021 April 6). Centers for Disease Control and Prevention. https://www.cdc.gov/violenceprevention/aces/fastfact.html?CDC_AA_refVal=https%3A%2F%2Fwww.cdc.gov%2Fviolenceprevention%2Facestudy%2Ffastfact.html

Franco, G. (n.d.) *How to deal with a narcissistic mother.* CBT Psychology. https://cbtpsychology.com/narcissisticmother/

Frank, D, L., Khorshid, L., Kiffer, J. F., Moravec, C. S., & McKee, M. G. (2010). Biofeedback in medicine: Who, when, why and how? *Mental Health in Family Medicine, 7*(2), 85-91.

Garrido, S., Baker, F. A., Davidson, J. W., Moore, G., & Wasserman, S. (2015). Music and trauma: The relationship between music, personality, and coping style. *Frontiers in Psychology*, 6, 977. doi:10.3389/fpsyg.2015.00977

Gibson, L. C. (2015 June 5). Parents who drive you crazy: Four steps for handling emotionally immature parents. *Huff Post.* https://www.huffpost.com/entry/parents-who-drive-you-cra_b_7511242

Gilbertson, M. W., Shenton, M. E., Ciszewski, A., Kasai. K., Lasko, N. B., Orr, S. P., & Pitman, R. K. (2010). Smaller hippocampal volume predicts pathologic vulnerability to psychological trauma. *Natural Neuroscience*, 5(11), 1242-1247. https://doi.org/10.1038/nn958

Goff, B. [@bobgoff]. (2018 May 21). *"We're all rough drafts of the people we're still becoming."* [Tweet]. Twitter. https://twitter.com/bobgoff/status/998565085701226496?lang=en

*Grey matter vs white matter in the brain.* (2020 June 7). Spinal Cord. https://www.spinalcord.com/blog/gray-matter-vs-white-matter-in-the-brain

Lancer, D. (2018 August 28). *Are your parents toxic?* Psych Central.

Lenz, A. S., & Roscoe, L. J. (2011). Personal wellness card sort: A strategy for promoting relational healing. *Journal of Creativity in Mental Health*, 6(1), 69-83. http://dx.doi.org/10.1080/15401383.2011.562755

Moore, C. (2021 June 16). *Positive daily affirmations: Is there science behind it?* Positive Psychology. https://positivepsychology.com/daily-affirmations/

Park, A. T., Leonard, J. A., Saxler, P. K., Cyr, A. B., Gabrieli, J. D. E., & Mackey, A. P. (2018). Amygdala-medial prefrontal cortex connectivity relates to stress and mental health in early childhood. *Social Cognitive and Affective Neuroscience*, 13(4), 430-439. https://doi.org/10.1093/scan/nsy017

*Positive feedback.* (2016 March). American Psychological Association. https://www.apa.org/monitor/2016/03/cover-feedback

*Prefrontal cortex.* (n.d.). American Psychological Association. https://dictionary.apa.org/prefrontal-cortex

Quirke, M. G. (n.d.) *What are the 10 ACEs of trauma & how can you begin to face them?* Michael G Quirke. https://michaelgquirke.com/what-are-the-10-aces-of-trauma-how-can-you-begin-to-face-them/

Riopel, L. (2021 November 2). *Resilience Skills, factors, and strategies of the resilient person.* Positive Psychology. https://positivepsychology.com/Resilience-Skills/

*Risk and protective factors*. (2021 January 5). Centers for Disease Control and Prevention. https://www.cdc.gov/violenceprevention/aces/riskpr otectivefactors.html

Robinson, L., Smith, M., & Segal, J. ( 2020 February). *Emotional and psychological trauma*. Help Guide. https://www.helpguide.org/articles/ptsd-trauma/coping-wit h-emotional-and-psychological-trauma.htm

Smith, J. A. (2014 November 26). Can giving thanks help us heal from trauma? *Greater Good Magazine*. https://greatergood.berkeley.edu/art icle/item/can_giving_thanks_help_heal_from_trauma

Spector, N. (2018 June 5). Mental health services: How to get treatment if you can't afford it. *NBC News-*. https://www.nbcnews.com/better/health/mental-health-services-h ow-get-treatment-if-you-can-t-ncna875176

Starecheski, Laura. (2015 March 2). Take the ACE quiz - and learn what it does and doesn't mean. *National Public Radio-*. https://www.npr.org/sections/health-shots/2015/03/02/387007941 /take-the-ace-quiz-and-learn-what-it-does-and-doesnt-mean

Tugade, M. M., Fredrickson, B. L., & Barrett, L. F. (2004). Psychological resilience and positive emotional granularity: Examining the benefits of positive emotions on coping and health. *Journal of Personality*, 72(6), 1161-1190. https://doi.org/10.111/j.1467-6494.2004.00294.x

*Violence prevention*. (2021 January 5). Centers for Disease Control and Prevention. https://www.cdc.gov/violenceprevention/aces/riskprotec tivefactors.html

*Vital signs*. (2019 November 5). Centers for Disease Control and Prevention. https://www.cdc.gov/vitalsigns/aces/index.html

*What are eating disorders?* (n.d.) American Psychiatric Association. https://www.psychiatry.org/patients-families/eating-di sorders/what-are-eating-disorders

*What is cognitive behavioral therapy?* (2017 July). American Psychological Association. https://www.apa.org/ptsd-guideline/patients-and-families/cognitive-behavioral

*What is depression?* (n.d.). American Psychiatric Association. https://www.psychiatry.org/patients-families/depression/what-is-depression

*What is EMDR?* (n.d.). EMDR Institute, Inc. https://www.emdr.com/what-is-emdr/

All images have been sourced by https://themartinsburginitiative.com/adverse-childhood-experiences/

Made in United States
North Haven, CT
25 August 2023

40746533R00065